CW00742836

UNDERGROUND HERITAGE

Tokens of Yesterday
on today's Tube

Antony Badsey-Ellis

Capital Transport

Photo credits

Antony Badsey-Ellis
10 centre left, 11, 13, 14, 22, 26, 27, 36, 50 left, 51 bottom, 54 left, 55, 56 left, 60 bottom, 71 bottom left, 75, 80, 81, 82, 83, 85, 86, 87 left, 88, 89, 90, 91, 92, 93, 95 top, 104, 106, 108, 116 left, 124, 125 left, 128, 129, 130, 133, 138, 139, 140, 141 top left, 142 bottom right, 143.

Kim Rennie
4

Other photographs are © Capital Transport

ISBN 978 185414 360 0

First published 2012
Published by
Capital Transport Publishing Ltd
www.capitaltransport.com

Printed by 1010 Printing International Ltd

Contents

UNDERGROUND
TO THE TRAINS
Way out

Introduction

Over the 150 years of its existence, the London Underground has continuously developed, extended, refreshed, and renewed itself. The twenty-first century in particular has seen massive investment in station modernization, initially through the ill-fated Public-Private Partnership. This proved to be a costly failure, and now that Transport for London fully controls the network the modernization projects have been restarted.

Such work has been carried out with due regard for the preservation or re-creation of the most significant or aesthetically pleasing aspects of the system's design history. Much survives from the tube boom of the Edwardian period, including a number of complete buildings listed by English Heritage or local authorities. These have been well covered elsewhere. This book mostly focuses on the details of the Underground's architectural heritage.

The large number of extensions built in the 1920s and 1930s led to new décor schemes around the network. At the same time the conversion of many stations to have escalators in place of lifts caused stations to be retiled. Inevitably interesting features were lost in these processes, but at the same time new features were added which today we see as being important parts of the Underground's heritage.

When I started to write this book I was surprised to find so many heritage items still in existence, even at modernized stations. The intent is to show only those features that can still be found around the Underground today; of course, a handful might have been removed since the photographs were taken as the station upgrade work continues.

The following pages show a selection of the heritage items, and group them by theme. Some photographs show more than one feature, and these are cross-referenced in the text where necessary.

Taking the many hundreds of photographs necessary for compiling this book has involved much footwork around the Underground, and my thanks go to Jim Whiting for his help with this. I also thank my wife, Wendy, for her support during my research and writing.

Antony Badsey-Ellis
Amersham, September 2012

Opposite: A sign dating from the 1920s at Clapham Common station.

SUB-SURFACE TILING

The City & South London Railway opened in 1890, linking Stockwell in south London with a station near the Monument called King William Street. Although the trains were electrically powered, the generating station at the railway's depot in Stockwell did not have capacity to power electric lighting at the six stations, which therefore used the inferior illumination of gas lights. It was essential to maximize the light provided, and hence glazed white tiles were used on platform walls.

The main tiles were 6 inches square and white, covering the subways and platform walls. Towards the floor were a few bands of ruby-coloured tiles, and at waist height was a decorative band. This consisted of three rows of tiles, each 6 inches wide by 3 inches high. The upper and lower bands were ruby or brown; the centre band contained an Arts and Crafts style fleur-de-lis pattern.

By the time of the Euston extension, the patterned band had been dropped, and the only decoration comprised two closely-spaced bands (one thin above one twice the thickness) along the walls.

Much of the original tiling was lost in the 1920s when the original sections of the C&SLR were reconstructed with longer platforms and larger tunnels. Stations from Borough southwards were retiled in the latest style (see p14). However, sections remained in passageways made redundant by the installation of escalators, as well as at City Road station, closed in 1922. The original white tiles on the curved ceilings of many platforms were also left *in situ* at some stations.

Today the only original tiling on display to the public is on the short set of stairs at the foot of the spiral staircase at Elephant & Castle station (right). The lowest part of the stairs from the platform has replica tiling, but the majority (up to the bottom of the spiral stairs) is original. Original tiling also still exists in closed areas at Kennington, as well as at City Road and King William Street disused stations.

Although the City & South London Railway had been transporting passengers underground for nearly a decade when the Central London Railway (part of today's Central Line) opened, the latter railway still caused a stir. The tunnels were larger, and better lit, and the white tiling throughout gave them a clean and bright appearance.

The tiles were of a white opal glass, known as Opalite, which was manufactured by the National Opalite Glazed Brick and Tile Syndicate Ltd, a British company founded in the 1890s. They reflected the light from the arc lamps to maximize the illumination available to passengers.

The tiles were also very hard wearing and easy to clean, and were described in one contemporary report as "having a granulated back incorporated in the glass which forms such a key that when fixed the plate and structure become one". Tiles wouldn't be falling off the walls of CLR stations in a hurry.

This point was proved by the longevity of the tiling. It was still in place at many stations decades later - even the very busy stations. Tottenham Court Road's for example lasted until the mid-1980s. The original tiles are still on the ceiling of Lancaster Gate and Chancery Lane stations, and are in reasonable condition given their age.

The opening of 46 new stations in 1906-7 by the Underground Electric Railways Company of London (UERL) was an impressive achievement. Even more impressive was the tiling on the 94 new platforms. Each was decorated with coloured tiles laid in repeating geometric patterns, and incorporating the station name at three points. Decorative signs indicating the platform exits were included, and tiled bands regularly wrapped themselves over the ceiling vault.

The tiling took up a length of wall totalling around six miles, and yet was designed manufactured, and fixed in position within a period of just over two years. The designer has not been recorded, but the evidence suggests a strong likelihood of it being the UERL's architect, Leslie Green.

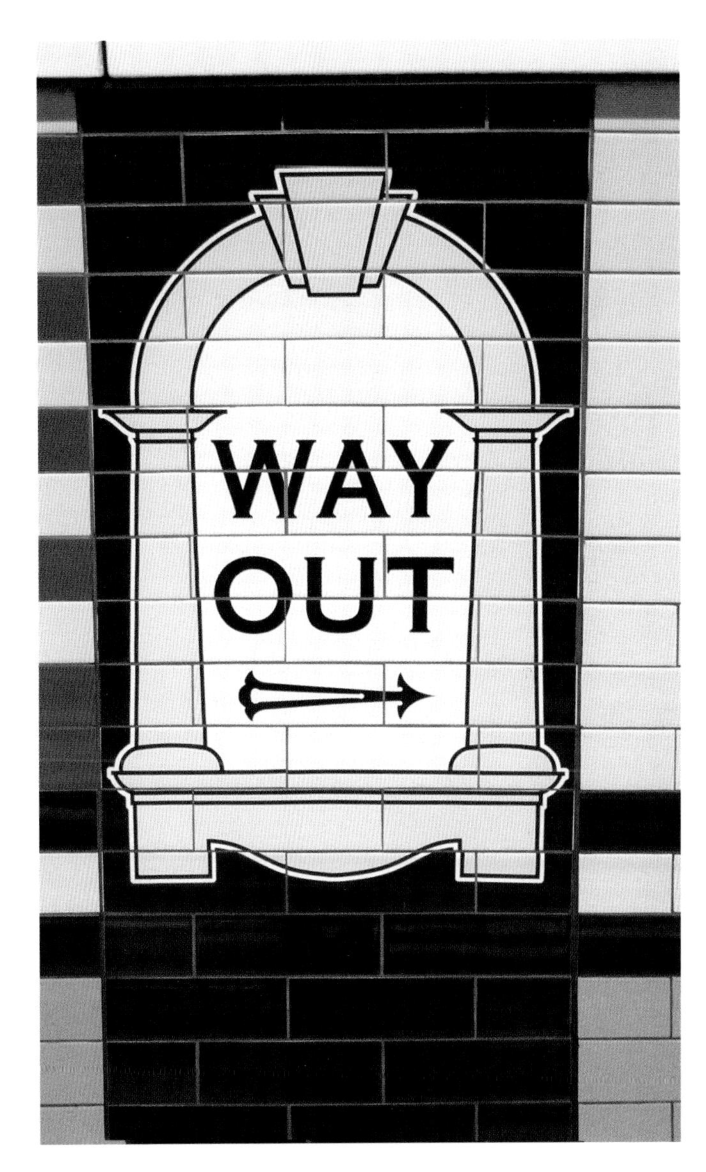

Many of the UERL stations with original tiling remaining in 2000 have had this replicated. This tiled sign is at Arsenal.

Replica Edwardian tiling was provided at Gloucester Road in 2007-8.

The tiles were supplied by three main manufacturers, but were all of the same dimensions, namely 9 × 3 inches. The tiling generally consisted of a tiled plinth four tiles high, with a section of plain tiling, often in cream above, and usually nine tiles high. There then followed a tiled waistband (the height varied between stations), with the geometric pattern above this for at least eleven rows of tiles. The later stations omitted the lower plain tiling in favour of cement render onto which advertising and posters could be stuck.

Over the years the stations began to be retiled, and the original patterns appeared to be lost. Painstaking research in the 1970s and 1980s recorded the remaining patterns and determined almost all of the lost patterns. Stations have continued to be refurbished, but in recent years the trend has been to replicate the original tiling; this has occurred with varying degrees of success. Part of the problem is that modern tiles have far better quality control: a batch of tiles can be made with all of them being uniformly the same colour. Back

Russell Square also has replacement tiling, with the enamelled name frieze interrupted for the tiled signs.

in 1906, the colour would vary depending on the quantity of glaze applied (by hand) and even the position of the tile in the kiln. The slight difference in colour from tile to tile was part of the attraction, and it is gratifying that this has been recognized and some stations have replica tiles that are designed with slight colour variations. The grouting width is another issue at some stations, being rather wider and therefore more noticeable than it was originally. This is due in part to the over-zealous adherence to modern tiling standards.

Some of the retiled stations have lost their patterns, but retain (new) tiled name panels and a coloured waistband. This started with Edgware Road (Bakerloo) in the 1990s, and Mornington Crescent and Camden Town have followed. Fortunately most of the replicas have since included the pattern, and have also tiled over the lower cement panels (at stations where this was provided). This gives greater consistency, if not historical authenticity.

TO FINSBURY PARK

TO HAMMERSMITH

TO THE TRAINS
TO FINSBURY PARK

This stairway has 193 steps
Do not use except in an emergency
TO THE STAIRS
Covent Garden station
This staircase
has 193

TO THE LIFTS & STAIRS

Way out

Above: Passageways and staircases at UERL stations were tiled in the same colours as their platforms. This shows the style of tiling adopted on spiral staircases, in this case at Regent's Park

Opposite top: The UERL stations incorporated tiled signs that, over time, were removed or covered over as the lines were extended and stations modified. These are from Holloway Road (left) and Gloucester Road (right).

Opposite centre: Holloway Road and Covent Garden.

Opposite bottom left: The mosaic tiling above the sign is not original, but added to make removal of graffiti easier.

Opposite bottom right: Golders Green was the only surface-level UERL station to receive any Leslie Green tiling. It has recently been replicated as shown here.

After the opening of the three UERL lines in the period 1906-1907 there was a short period of stasis on the Underground, during which time attention was focused on working together and co-ordinating fares and signs. The Bakerloo Tube continued its slow expansion westwards to Queen's Park and the Hampstead Tube was extended one station south from its terminus at Charing Cross to meet the District Railway at the station known today as Embankment. A single platform on a loop was provided, and this received a different style of décor to that which had gone before. Raised turquoise tiles formed borders around station name signs and poster sites, with flat tiles in the same colour forming a plinth to the floor, and also joining adjacent sites together. A continuous strip of these tiles, bounded top and bottom by the ridged tiles, ran at frieze height along the platform. Alternate roundel name signs were placed higher up on the wall, presumably to make it easier for passengers to see the station name if the platform was crowded. Similar tiles were used for the poster sites along the interchange subway to the Bakerloo platforms. These remain in situ, unlike the platform tiling, which was replaced in 1987.

The three Bakerloo stations north of Paddington opened in 1915, and received similar tiling to Embankment, although the bands of flat tiles do not seem to have had the decorative treatment used at Embankment, with the alternating pairs of tiles placed horizontally and vertically.

These stations have been refurbished in the past few years, but the tiling has remained similar. Warwick Avenue remains most authentic, although the continuous turquoise strip has been covered over by the name frieze. The tiling at Maida Vale has been replaced in a similar style, but with inset frames of red and blue, somewhat detracting from the original look. The portals accessing the lower escalator concourse have been painted a similar shade of green, although were white when the stations opened, and the portal decoration has been removed (see p130).

Opposite: The long passageway between the Bakerloo and Northern lines at Embankment showing the tiling from 1914.

Warwick Avenue, 1915.

Maida Vale, showing the replica chequerboard tiling on walls and columns.

JIMMY CARR
OUT ON DVD NOW
0800 716 543
AND I DON'T NEED
THESE GLASSES ANYMORE!

In the 1920s the City & South London Railway tunnels, originally constructed with diameters as small as 10 ft 2 ins, were enlarged to accommodate what had become the standard size of rolling stock on the Underground. This would allow through running with the Hampstead Tube, planned as far back as 1913 but delayed by the onset of the First World War. The complete rebuilding of the line, together with the extension of the station platforms so that longer trains could be operated, meant that the stations required complete redecoration.

The style chosen continued to rely heavily on plain white tiles, although these tended to have a slight blue/grey tinge to them. The sites for posters and the name roundels were framed by turquoise-green, silver-grey, dark green, and then black tiles; as with the stations built in the previous decade, alternate roundels were placed at higher level. A plinth in very dark maroon tiles was provided along the length of the platforms at each station.

As well as the reconstructed stations adopting this style, all of the new stations on the southward extension to Morden and the connecting line between Kennington and Embankment followed suit. Other stations rebuilt at the same time also acquired this tiling, including St James's Park, Embankment (District line), and Blackfriars. St James's Park has not been modernised, and shows today the effect of this tiling on a sub-surface station.

Many of the original Northern line stations on the line to Morden have been retiled in the original style in the past decade. The tiles from the 1920s had been damaged over the years, and a lack of maintenance had taken its toll. The replacements look good, but they are not quite the same. Greater consistency in the colouring of tiles has removed the slight but attractive variation in colour in the white and black tiles; compare the photographs of Colliers Wood and Oval to see the difference.

The entrance stairwells at Aldgate East feature the same blue tiled edging used on the platforms.

The 1920s tiling scheme was also applied to staircases and passageways at stations, as seen here at Camden Town

A change of style occurred in the 1930s. For the first time on the Underground, the predominant colour was not white, but a creamy colour usually described as 'biscuit'. Improvements in lighting technology meant that the platforms no longer needed highly glazed white tiles. It was perhaps thought that tiles of this colour would show the dirt and dust slightly less as well. The tiles were square.

On the Piccadilly Line extension north of Finsbury Park, coloured highlights were placed around the arched entrances to the sub-surface platforms, poster sites and in a band along the top and bottom of the main tiling. Each station received a different colour: blue at Manor House, yellow at Turnpike Lane, green and cream stripes at Wood Green, red at Bounds Green, and yellow at Southgate.

Manor House, 1932

The green and brown tiled bands either side of the name frieze at Swiss Cottage represented the Metropolitan and Bakerloo lines which both served this station at its opening in 1939.

Highgate, opened in 1941, was given three bands of green tiles.

From 1937, the name of each tube tunnel station began to be added as a frieze along the top line of the tiling. Following experiments using paper, the frieze was fired into the tiles in black lettering using the Johnston typeface on a biscuit background. Successive repetitions of the name were separated by red and blue roundels, also fired into the tiles. Lines of coloured tiles ran above and below the frieze, and black tiles were used around poster sites and in a band immediately above the black plinth tiling.

Swiss Cottage received green and brown lines, whilst at St John's Wood the bands were yellow and brown. The new Metropolitan line platforms at King's Cross used green and black, Bethnal Green used red and black, and St Paul's and Aldgate East were blue. The latter station also used blue tiling around poster sites and in a single band along the top edge of the plinth.

On the Northern line, Highgate station had plain green bands for the frieze, poster edging, and plinth band; the same colour scheme was used at Wanstead on the Central line. Redbridge was the same, but with blue tiles, and Gants Hill used yellow.

Many of these tiles have now been replaced with modern facsimiles during modernization work, with varying degrees of success. The tile edges and grouting width at Swiss Cottage and St John's Wood have spoiled the effect of the original, but other stations have rectified these problems by using narrower grouting lines. The work at Turnpike Lane station, a listed building, has been commended by English Heritage, whilst following the completion of refurbishment work at Bounds Green the station was given a Grade II listing. Research conducted by LU during the work revealed that the red colour in the glaze used at Bethnal Green was due in part to depleted uranium.

In 1936 the LPTB commissioned the artist and craftsman Harold Stabler to design eighteen ceramic tiles to decorate the walls of new and refurbished Underground stations. Stabler, who was a friend of Frank Pick, created tiles which included the counties around London, four buildings, and two emblems of London Transport (LT). The tiles are six inches square, matching the plain 'biscuit' tiles used in conjunction with them.

Stabler's tiles, made at the Carter & Company Pottery in Poole, were first used when Aldgate East station was rebuilt in 1938. St Paul's station was rebuilt and retiled in the same year using the new tiles. They were used subsequently at St John's Wood, Swiss Cottage, and one platform at Baker Street, for the Bakerloo line extension in 1939; the first two of these platforms received all tile designs. The eastern extension of the Central line made use of them at Bethnal Green, Wanstead, Redbridge, and Gants Hill. The latter three stations used only the roundel tile, but decorated in red and blue.

Baker Street lost its tiles when the platform was retiled for the Jubilee line in 1979, and St Paul's was retiled in 1986. Wanstead, St John's Wood, and Swiss Cottage have been retiled but with replicas of the original Stabler tiles in recent years, and manufactured by the Staffordshire firm of H&E Smith.

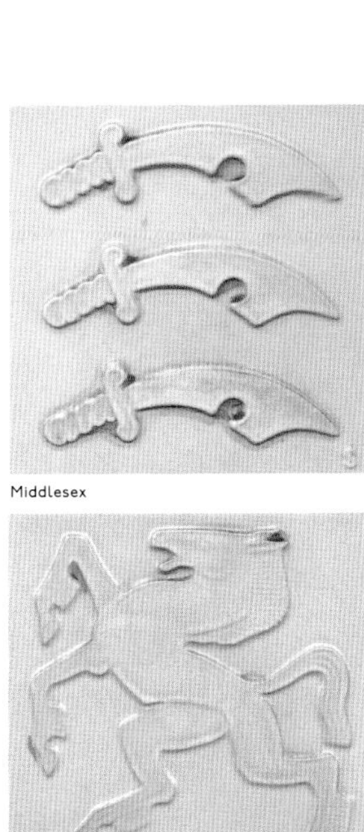
Middlesex

Hertfordshire

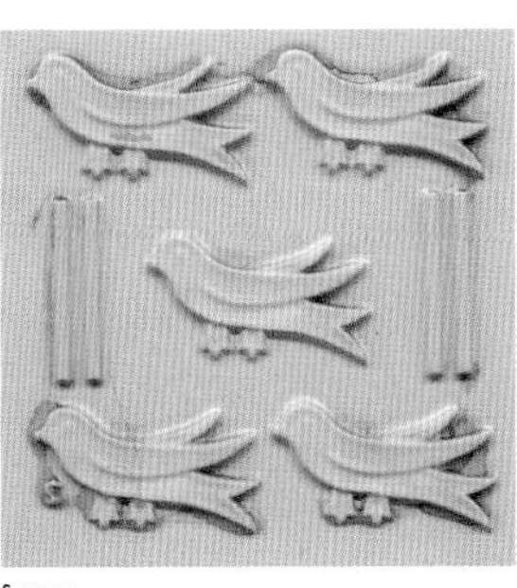
Sussex

Bedfordshire

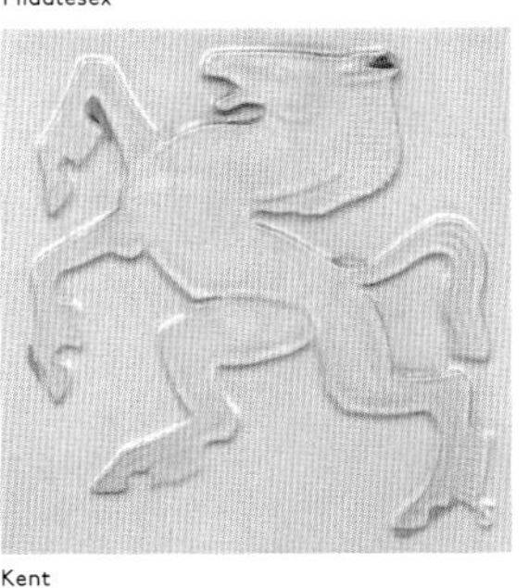
Kent

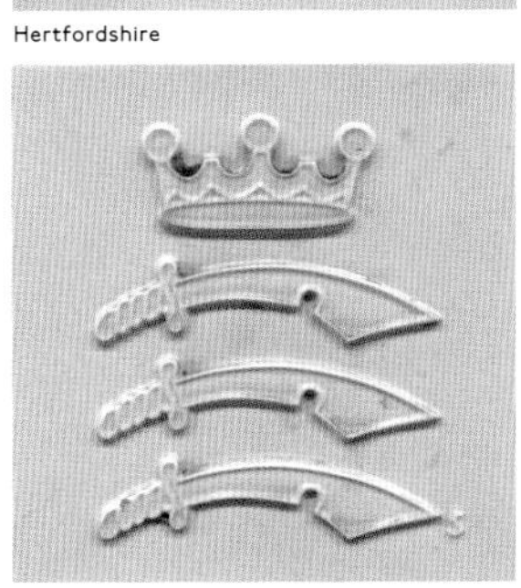
Essex

County of London

Surrey

Buckinghamshire

Berkshire

Crystal Palace

Griffin

St Paul's

London's River

Thomas Lord

Parliament

The stations opened on the Victoria line all had a common feel, which one commentator described as belonging to the 'late lavatorial' style. The extensive use of square grey tiles on the platform and trackside walls was the cause of this remark. The stations were enlivened only by the advertisements pasted on the walls, and the creation of tiled motifs in each of the seating areas, each motif having a connection with the station.

The wall recesses at Victoria show the Queen's silhouette above the simple wooden benches. The metal handrails are a more recent addition.

WALTHAMSTOW CENTRAL (*by Julia Black*) is based on a design by the artist William Morris, who lived locally.

BLACKHORSE ROAD (*Hans Unger*) shows a simple drawing of a black horse, head on.

TOTTENHAM HALE (*Edward Bawden*) depicts the ferry which used to take people across the nearby River Lea.

SEVEN SISTERS (*Hans Unger*) is a slightly abstract depiction of the seven trees from which the locality takes its name.

FINSBURY PARK (*Tom Eckersley*) used to be a popular place for duelling, hence the crossed pistols.

HIGHBURY & ISLINGTON (*Edward Bawden*) had a castle (or 'high bury') which was destroyed during the peasant's revolt in 1381.

KING'S CROSS ST PANCRAS (*Tom Eckersley*) is a pattern of crossed made up of crowns, hence a play on King's Cross.

EUSTON (*Tom Eckersley*) is a reminder of the famous Doric propylæum which welcomed passengers to the main-line station until its destruction in 1961/2.

WARREN STREET (*Crosby/Fletcher/Forbes*) shows a maze or warren, being the second motif based on word play.

OXFORD CIRCUS (*Hans Unger*) is an abstract representation of the circus (as a white circle) with either the roads above, or the tube lines below. After a major fire in 1984 which resulted in complete redecoration of the platforms a new motif was used, matching that on the adjacent Bakerloo line. Redecoration in 2009 has now restored the original tiled motif (although a solitary panel from the 1980s tiling remains).

GREEN PARK (*Hans Unger*) is another abstract motif, based on an aerial view of the trees in the park.

VICTORIA (*Edward Bawden*) shows a silhouette of that Queen.

PIMLICO (*Peter Sedgley*) has an abstract design for the nearby Tate Gallery.

VAUXHALL (*George Smith*) has a reminder of the ornamental ironwork at the Vauxhall Gardens, which used to be nearby.

STOCKWELL (*Abram Games*) shows an abstract swan, for the nearby public house of that name.

BRIXTON (*Hans Unger*) is the third word-play motif, depicting a 'ton' of 'bricks'.

Way out →
VAUXHALL
Way out →

Way out →
STOCKWELL
Way out →

WARREN STREET

EUSTON
Way out →

When the Jubilee line opened in 1979, it added only seven new platforms to the Underground. Charing Cross, Green Park, and Bond Street each gained two platforms, whilst Baker Street only needed one additional platform for northbound trains. Even though their number was small, they were very different in style from those that had been decorated previously. Bright colours and bold designs were used to herald the newest line in London. The platforms at Charing Cross closed in 1999 when the line was extended from Green Park to Stratford, but they are regularly used for filming and television.

Red tiles were originally planned for the new Jubilee line platforms, with the designs being a later addition. This explains the odd appearance of Green Park.

The tiling of the Jubilee line platforms at Bond Street reflects the nearby shopping streets.

Probably the most famous (albeit fictional) resident of Baker Street appears in the tiling of that station. The Bakerloo line platform tiling shown here dates from 1981.

STREET LEVEL TILING

The attractive gilded lettering at Russell Square station is original. The letters are tightly kerned, and as a result the tiles have irregular edges to allow the letters to fit together.

All of the stations designed by Leslie Green had their names displayed on the façade using raised letters. They opened within two years of each other and four distinct styles were used. The friezes were located in two bands: between the ground and first storeys, and below the roofline.

The earliest style was gilded lettering raised from ox-blood tiles. All of these friezes used a serif typeface, which could be wide or condensed according to the space available. The tiles were made specifically for each name, as they were shaped to allow slight overlaps between the letters.

The next style appears to be in a similar typeface, but using raised black letters on a white background. Perhaps the visibility of the station names needed to be improved, and hence the change? This was used at only six stations though; most of the remainder used the black lettering on a white background, but in a sans-serif block typeface. Like the gilded tiles, both wide and condensed forms were used. The fourth style was uniquely used at Holborn, which had a distinctive stonework façade to better match the new buildings on Kingsway. White block lettering was used for this station.

On the Bakerloo Tube, almost all of the original stations placed their names on the lower frieze, and used gilt lettering on an ox-blood background. The two exceptions were the Jermyn Street façade for Piccadilly Circus station and Westminster Bridge Road (now Lambeth North), which both used the black serif tiles. The latter station was renamed less than five months after opening. A photograph of the original façade has not been found, but so this might have used the gilded lettering at first. Waterloo was a one-off, using a more ornate serif typeface.

All of these Bakerloo stations also showed the full name of the company on the upper frieze. This was in gilded metal lettering, with a similar (but not identical) typeface to the station names. Again, Waterloo appears to be the exception, using tiled letters in the same typeface as the name.

The other exception on the Bakerloo was Edgware Road, the last station to be opened. This used the black block lettering, and placed the station name on the upper frieze and the railway name on the lower frieze.

Covent Garden is one of the best remaining examples of the black and white seriffed lettering.

TILED ALPHABETS

The partial alphabets on these two pages have been compiled from the frieze lettering tiles still present on stations today. On the left hand page the two alphabets used by the UERL in 1906-7 are shown. Each tile appears to have been moulded for a specific station, rather than the pottery making a set of letters for use. This allowed the lettering to be spaced appropriately for each frieze. This has also resulted in a variety of letterforms: compare, for example, the three different S's in the block alphabet. Both typefaces employed normal and condensed lettering, the latter being used for narrow friezes. Caledonian Road station also used a unique tile with the abbreviation $\mathrm{R^{D}}$ to fit a single bay of the façade.

The right hand page shows (top right) the lettering used by the UERL's architect, Stanley Heaps, on his Bakerloo line extension stations of 1915. He designed these in a similar style to the existing tube stations of Leslie Green, with façades of red-glazed terracotta. They were only one storey high, and so were only able to accommodate a single band of frieze lettering. The letters are more consistent than on the earlier stations, but in style resemble the seriffed lettering used by Green. Another difference is the use of larger initial capital letters for each word. The limited selection of letters is a consequence of this typeface being used at only two stations (Maida Vale and Kilburn Park).

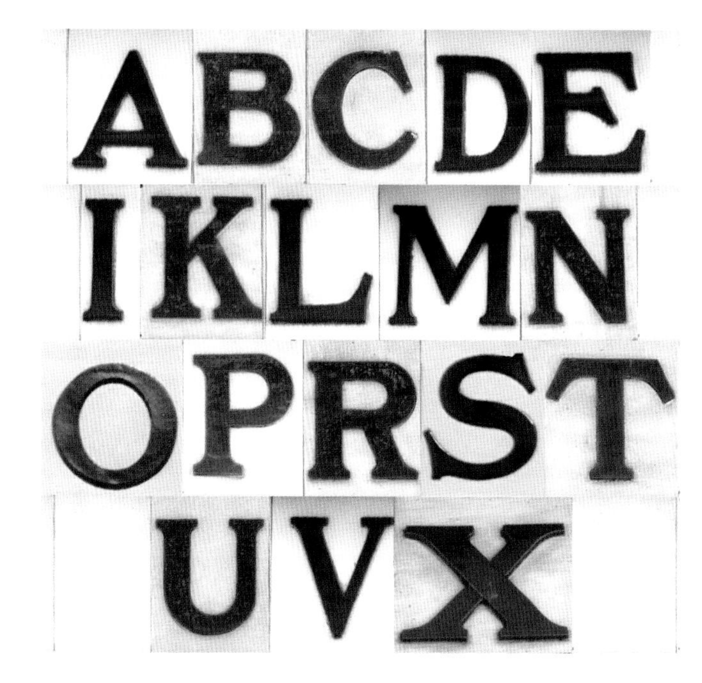

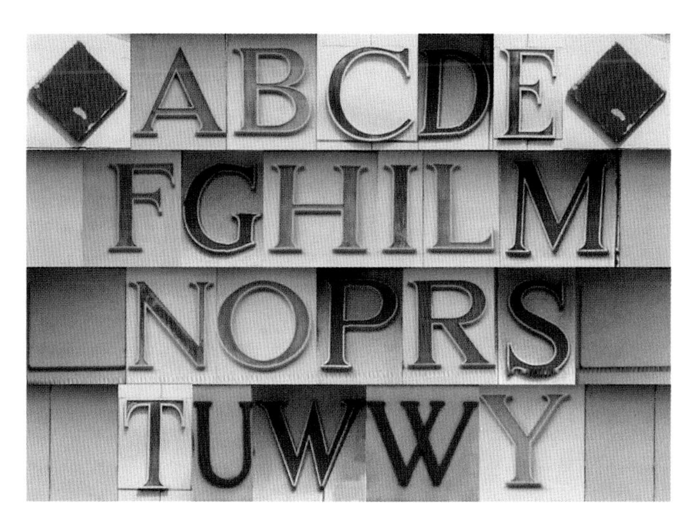

Left are the letters employed on the Metropolitan Railway stations rebuilt in the 1920s. Two slightly different types of tile were used. The friezes below the station cornice have letters with raised edges; some have been painted over the years, resulting in the variations of colour. The other tiles were used elsewhere, for example, to name the offices above the station at Edgware Road (see p135). These omitted the edges and hence appear to be of one colour. Note also the two different styles of 'W' used, both at Edgware Road station. Also shown with these tiles are the MR diamond, still visible above the entrance at Farringdon, and an unpainted raised square, used at each end of some friezes.

Tiled signs showing the new UNDERGROUND branding were applied to stations from 1908.

The Piccadilly Tube stations were more varied than those of the other lines. Stations from Gillespie Road (now Arsenal) to Russell Square spelt out their names using the gilded tiled lettering. Only Holloway Road gave the line name (as initials), probably because its façade was wide enough to be able to do this. Dover Street (now Green Park), Down Street, Brompton Road, and Gloucester Road were the same. Covent Garden and South Kensington used the black on white serif with the name on the lower frieze; Knightsbridge and Leicester Square were the same, but with the station name on the upper frieze. The latter featured the line names (Piccadilly & Hampstead) on the lower frieze, probably because it was one of the few interchange stations. The line names used the block typeface, giving a slightly disjointed effect on the station façade.

Hyde Park Corner and Strand (now Aldwych) stations used only the block typeface, placing the station name on the lower frieze. At Aldwych, the line name was placed on the upper frieze on both façades.

By contrast to the other two lines, the Hampstead Tube was very straightforward. All of its stations used the black block typeface for both station and line name, and the line name always appeared on the lower frieze. Station names appeared on the upper frieze, with the only exception (there had to be one) being Euston, where both line and station name shared the lower frieze.

The station at Aldwych closed in 1994, and the removal of the entrance canopy revealed the original station name. These two photographs show the sans-serif lettering. The upper friezes originally read PICCADILLY TUBE; this was changed around 1908 as the word 'tube' fell out of favour.

Mornington Crescent shows the unusual letterform of the 'G', appearing almost like a 'C'. The word 'STATION' has had its 'T's transposed during refurbishment, giving it an irregular appearance.

These tiled signs were provided at Maida Vale and Kilburn Park stations, both opened in 1915 on the Bakerloo line.

Earl's Court has these attractive tiled names on the Earl's Court Road façade, designed by Harry Ford for the MDR and opened in 1906.

Harry Ford also designed the MDR building at Barons Court, opened in 1905, and featuring the station and company names on faience blocks.

The modernisation of many Metropolitan Railway stations in the period from 1914 to 1931 followed a new house style, and was created by the company architect Charles W. Clark. Stations were rebuilt with exteriors clad in biscuit-coloured faience, and frieze lettering was used to prominently display both the name of the station and the company. The green letters were cast into the faience tiles and, unlike the UERL, were of a consistent seriffed typeface. The only decoration on the friezes comprised small diamonds, as used by the Metropolitan on name signs and other features - e.g. see clock on page 108. The lettering remains on the stations at Farringdon (as illustrated on these two pages), Paddington, Willesden Green, Aldgate and Edgware Road.

FARRINGDON & HIGH HOLBORN STATION
FARRINGDON STATION
Farringdon: Past, Present and Future

ENTRANCE

MOSAICS

Mosaics have a long history on the Underground, both for decoration and for signs. Many are still extant, demonstrating their durability. Tiles wear better than paint or plasterwork, and smaller tiles provide greater scope for decorative effects, as the Romans knew over two millennia ago. Probably the most famous mosaics on the Underground are those at Tottenham Court Road, some of which are shown on page 37–8.

Two of the oldest mosaics in existence today on the Underground are at Gloucester Road station, forming a pair of signs that proudly proclaim the station ownership. They are thought to date from around 1906, being added when the Piccadilly Tube station opened next door, and were refurbished (along with the rest of the station) in the 1990s.

Mosaics have been used for the Underground roundel as well. Charing Cross (now Embankment) station originally bore such a design when reconstructed in 1914. The following year a pair of beautiful tiled roundels were provided above the entrance stairs at Maida Vale station, which was designed by the Underground group's architect, Stanley Heaps. In 1932 Gillespie Road station on the Piccadilly line was renamed Arsenal, at the suggestion of the nearby football club. The station was enlarged at the same time to allow it to handle better the traffic on match days, and its façade was completely altered from the glazed terracotta design of Leslie Green. In its place came a large, plain wall which featured an enormous mosaic roundel. This remains in place today, having been renewed in 1993 (see photograph on p55).

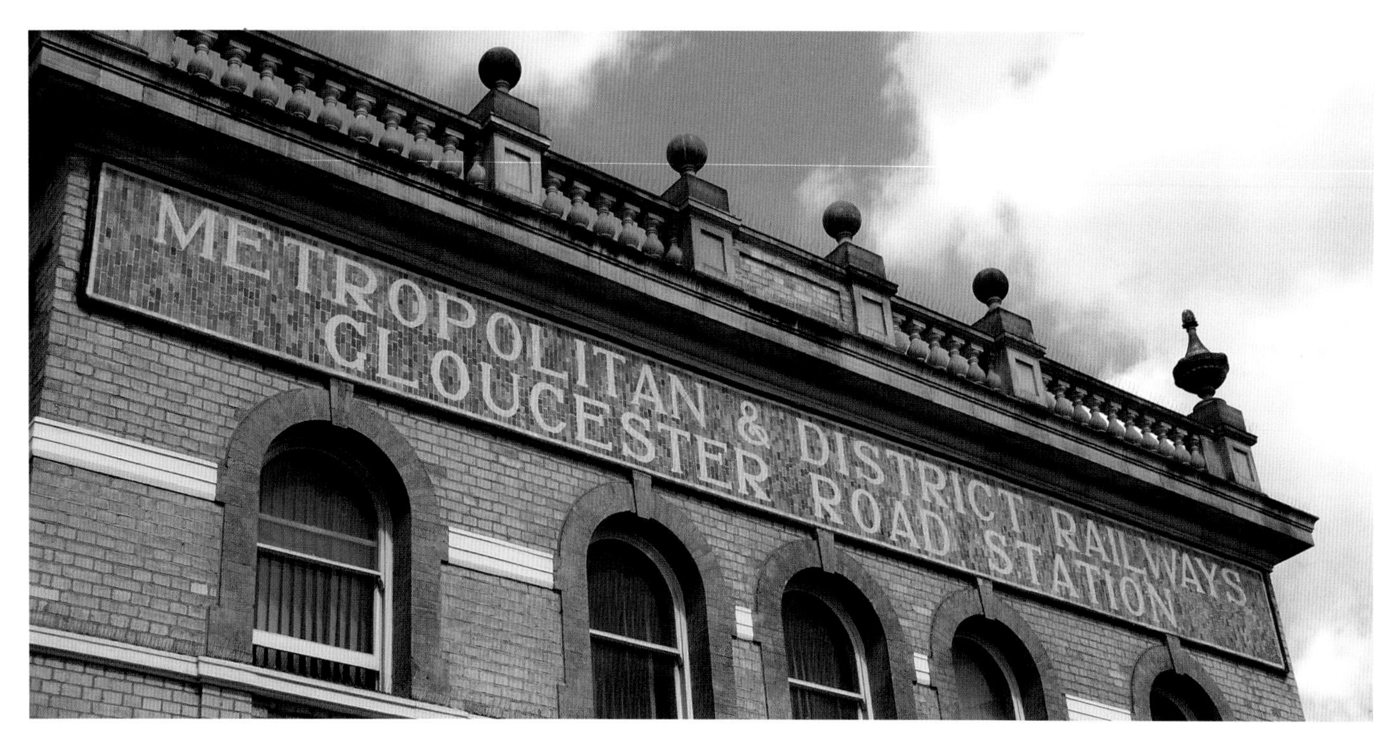

Maida Vale, 1915

Watford, 1925

The Metropolitan Railway stations designed by Charles W. Clark in the 1920s featured extensive mosaic tiling on walls in the ticket hall areas. Large areas were covered in green and turquoise tiles, and bands of purple and yellow, with an Metropolitan diamond motif provided more interest. This survives today at Aldgate, Edgware Road, Watford, Croxley, and Willesden Green, but has been lost at Swiss Cottage, St John's Wood Road, and Notting Hill Gate.

A humorous view of the complexity of Oxford Circus station, with its maze of underground passageways, appeared as a game of 'snakes and ladders' shown in mosaic tiling on the Central line platforms in 1983. Two years later the Bakerloo line platforms were completed with a different pattern, in green and white mosaic tiling. This time the design could be seen in two ways: passengers riding up and down a series of escalators, or as people lost in a three-dimensional maze. Both are appropriate interpretations capturing the confusing nature and geometry of the station. The designs for both lines were designed by the artist Nicholas Munro. The station was modernized between 2004 and 2009 and sadly the mosaics were removed. Only one single panel of each mosaic has been preserved on each line; the rest of the platforms have been retiled using large, plain white rectangular tiles.

Oxford Circus (Bakerloo line), 1985

One of the most unusually decorated and distinctive stations on the Underground is Tottenham Court Road. Originally the Central line platforms had plain white tiles, and those of the Northern line a pattern in cream and green. As part of the modernization programme started in the late 1970s, the artist Eduardo Paolozzi was commissioned to create designs for the central portions of each platform, with the remainder being tiled with thin cream tiles.

The mosaics reflected the vibrant street scenes around the station: late-night eateries, music publishers, electronics and computer shops, and the British Museum. Those on the Central line platforms are brighter and more colourful, with a noticeable use of warm colours (like the red used as the Central line colour). The Northern line mosaics are more monochrome; again, indicating the black colour used for the line, and the shared areas at the station (such as the interchange passageways) use a mixture.

The mosaics consist of a mixture of irregular tile fragments and small square tiles in various colours, all set against a background of square off-white tiles in a regular grid. Paolozzi's name appears in different places as well as the dates of completion.

The tiling was extended onto the ceiling, above the trunking carrying the cables and bearing the station name frieze, covering around 1,000 m^2. In the passageways it was more subdued, but bright colours were used on the unusual feature of a triple archway over the top of the main escalator shaft. At the foot of the escalators a polished metal ceiling was installed in the circular area known as the 'rotunda': actually, the bottom of one of the disused lift shafts. The only disjointed note is the square lighting installation, which does not fit with the circular space, and seems a remarkably odd choice given the attention to detail elsewhere in the station.

The decoration won a silver medal in the 1985 British Architectural Design Awards, and an exhibition about the design was held at the Royal Academy in 1986.

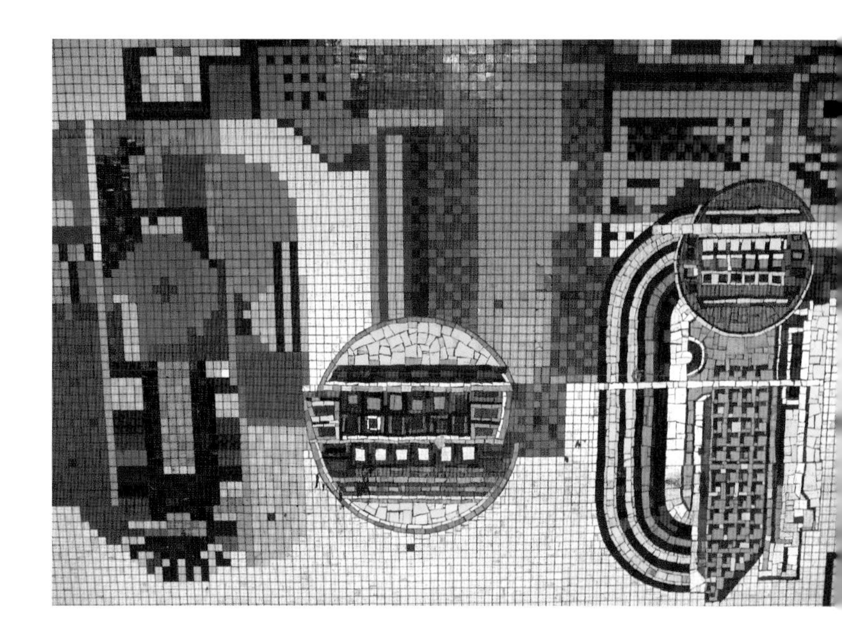

STOP
PUSH → ● ← PUSH

Another station to be given mosaic designs in the 1980s was Finsbury Park. The artist and designer Annabel Grey was commissioned to create a series of mosaics depicting hot-air balloons, reflecting the open space and parkland nearby. The balloons are placed on the trackside walls, wrapping up and onto the ceiling vaults.

TICKET HALLS

The upper band of tiles in the ticket hall at Barons Court uses this darker green circular motif (above).

The Underground retains a wide variety of ticket halls, with a few features dating back into the nineteenth century. All of the older halls have undergone various amount of alteration over the years, some more than others. This can be attributed to the construction of new lines, addition of escalators, and general modernization, but probably the single largest reason is the advances in ticketing technology. From the outset stations had rooms for clerks to work and sell tickets to passengers via a small window. The Underground was at the forefront of introducing new ticketing technology to speed passenger flows, with cinema-style Automaticket machines in use from the 1920s. Passimeters (see p112) moved staff onto the concourse of ticket halls, in some cases freeing up the space previously used for ticket offices. Free-standing passenger-operated ticket machines which required no staff were introduced gradually from the same decade, and rebuilt stations such as Piccadilly Circus received them in large numbers. This trend continued, with the machines evolving with time and passing trends of style.

The main ticketing event that transformed many ticket halls was the introduction of the Underground Ticketing System from 1987. All stations required new, secure ticket offices at the edge of the ticket hall, ticket machines required secure space behind for servicing, and new pneumatically operated ticket barriers were installed at Zone 1 stations. The ticket halls at some stations were changed beyond recognition, and many of the changes were to the detriment of the history of the station. Many of the stations in the outer zones were affected less as they continued to use manual ticket inspection, but the system-wide installation of automatic ticket gates from 1998 has meant that further alterations have been made.

Barons Court retains its beautiful green ceramic tiles, with darker green patterned tiles just beneath the ceiling, together with ceramic ticket windows and swan-necked illuminated signs. The latter are replicas, as for much of the period from the 1930s until the 1980s a passimeter was squeezed into the end of the ticket hall. Careful restoration work was carried out in the mid-1990s to restore as much as possible of the station to its original appearance.

Chalk Farm is one of the best survivors of the original UERL stations. These were tiled with large green tiles (darker than those at Barons Court) up to around head height, at which a tiled frieze was placed. At most stations this depicted either acanthus leaves or pomegranates. Above the frieze the walls were tiled or painted with tiled bands, as seen at Chalk Farm. Original metal railings protect the entrance to the spiral staircase here, but the ticket office windows are of a modern design in brushed steel. The Maxim arc lamps have been replaced by fluorescent lighting, but the handsome Self-Winding Clock (see p104) is still in the same place. Comparison with a photograph taken just after opening shows that the ticket hall layout has become considerably more cluttered in its century of opening.

Many of the UERL ticket halls have been completely rebuilt. Belsize Park, one stop north from Chalk Farm, retains no traces of its original features. However, recognition in the 1990s that heritage was worth preserving led to the recreation of original features when stations were refurbished. Mornington Crescent and Edgware Road (Bakerloo) stations have had their ticket halls rebuilt entirely, but in the style conceived by the architect, Leslie Green. The execution of the work is very good, but it must be remembered that they are pastiches.

Each decade of the inter-war period produced a different style of ticket hall, and many of these have been retained, although with modern additions. The extension of the Bakerloo line to Queen's Park added three new tube stations to the map, at Warwick Avenue, Maida Vale, and Kilburn Park. Although the latter had its ticket hall at street level, whereas the first two named had sub-surface halls, they shared a common style.

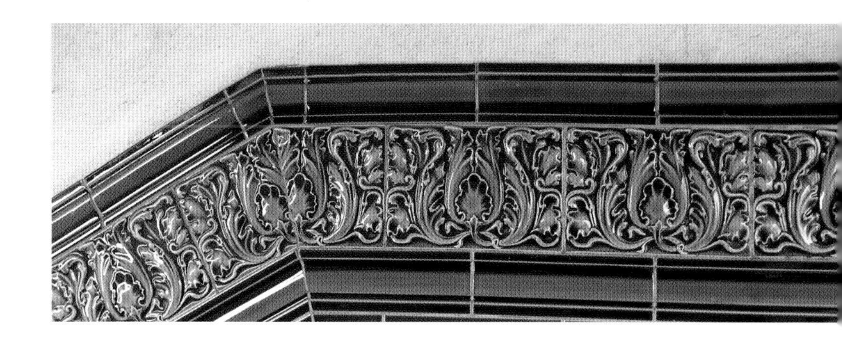

Regent's Park (1906) has the acanthus leaf tile frieze in the subway leading to the ticket hall (above right). The pomegranate tiling is still visible (right) at Chalk Farm station (1907).

Edgware Road station on the Bakerloo line was extensively refurbished in 1992. The ticket office windows, with their Art Nouveau lettering are perfect replicas of the 1907 originals, and the tiling has been restored.

An unusual and attractive pair of crossing staircases at Maida Vale. The yellow tint to the tiles is an artifact of the lighting; they are actually white.

The ticket hall at Maida Vale, dating from 1915, has retained its wooden ticket office windows. These were used by the UERL for later stations in place of the ceramic style shown opposite at Edgware Road.

These were an evolution of Leslie Green's UERL stations, but designed by the Underground Group's architect, Stanley Heaps, with ox-blood terracotta façades. In the ticket halls tiling was white, with a band of green and white chequered tiling above. The chequered tiling was also used as a border on the floors. Time took its toll on the tiling, and the inevitable changes to the ticket halls meant that retiling became inevitable. Fortunately the same style was retained for the walls, although the floors have been given a more standard finish with square biscuit-coloured tiles. Maida Vale also has an unusual arrangement of entrance and exit staircases that appear to intertwine as they descend from street level.

The extension of the Hampstead Line to Edgware in 1924 brought with it five new stations: Brent (now Brent Cross), Hendon Central, Colindale, Burnt Oak, and Edgware. These were designed by Stanley Heaps, and have been described as 'suburban classical' in appearance. The building at Colindale was destroyed by bombs in the Second World War, but the ticket halls at the other four stations have remained in good condition. Inside, the ticket halls have retained their black and white chequerboard quarry tile floors and many of the wooden and bronze fittings, including the impressive glazed wooden doors. Automatic ticket gates have been added, and modern lighting replaces the original incandescent bulbs, but much of the original 'feel' of these ticket halls remains.

Kilburn Park, 1915

The Metropolitan Railway was still independent from the Underground in the 1920s, and developed its own station styles. These can broadly be described as 'urban' and 'suburban', and both were designed by the company's architect, Charles W. Clark. Most of the 'urban' style, with their exteriors clad in pale faience, have had their ticket halls significantly altered over the last eighty years, and only fragments of heritage detail remain: see, for example, the green mosaic tiling at Willesden Green and Aldgate. Great Portland Street has a splendid roundel sign directing passengers to the platforms (see p100), as well as some original windows (now painted over) into the offices around the ticket hall. The ticket hall at Baker Street retains its faience-clad pillars (as do the Metropolitan line platforms) and gently-arched ceiling beams. Much of this was restored in the 1980s, having become rather gloomy and grimy over the previous years.

At the suburban stations, which resemble large Arts-and-Crafts houses, the small ticket halls retain their windows, doors, and mouldings at Croxley and Watford, but the original mosaic finishes at the former have been replaced by less attractive square green tiles. Fortunately Watford has kept large amounts of the mosaic (see p36).

The ticket halls for the seven stations opened in 1924 on the extension to Morden have all been retiled from their original white, black and green (see p14). Balham has been given an unpleasant pastiche which fails to match the quality of the original.

The largest number of listed stations on the Underground date from the 1930s, and were designed by Charles Holden. The northern extension of the Piccadilly line to Cockfosters

The Metropolitan Railway ticket hall at Baker Street was restored in 1987, and has kept its original signs above the modern facilities.

Manor House, 1932

provided eight completely new stations, whilst to the west of London around a dozen existing stations were entirely rebuilt. Outside, red brick walls were pierced by industrial metal-framed windows, and were surmounted by concrete roofs. Concrete was used for other features around the stations, including lamp posts and fences (see p124 and 138). Inside, the ticket halls in most cases are in reasonable heritage condition, allowing for modern lighting and ticketing-related changes. Manor House has a sub-surface ticket hall with an unusual ceiling consisting of concentric circles resembling ripples spreading outwards, with light fittings at the centre of some of the circles. Information panels (nearby bus routes, fares, etc.) are accommodated on enlarged pillars with bronze frames; sadly, the litter bins around the base of these have been removed for security reasons. Further north, Arnos Grove has a cylindrical ticket hall with a central passimeter (p115), from which a column rises to the high ceiling. The bronze fittings at the ticket hall windows remain in place, as do some of the opal glass light fixtures. Overall, this station remains very close to Holden's original vision. One station further north, at Southgate, also retains many similar heritage features, including the passimeter and bronze details, escalator uplighting (p123), and central passimeter. The kiosks around the edge of the building all use the Johnston typeface, matching the station signs, and opal glass light fixtures are again present. The lower panels around the hall have a geometric design in blue and white: the colours are not original, the panels being in bronze at the time of the station opening in 1933.

New stations opened in the 1940s were generally similar to those of the 1930s, having been planned at the same time but delayed in opening because of WWII. Little was changed in the 1950s, and it was only when the Victoria line opened in the late 1960s that a new design of ticket hall appeared. Like everything else on the new line, the ticket halls were designed to look modern and match the grey tiling used elsewhere on the stations. The line was built on a tight budget, and many of the stations have since been enlarged, with significant changes to their ticket halls. Pimlico, the last station to open on the line, has undergone little change. The ticket windows are in the same place, but the free-standing self-service machines that stood in angled rows in 1972 have been replaced by the ubiquitous wall-mounted UTS ticket machines. Likewise, the original ticket gates were replaced by UTS gates in 1988, but along the same line.

Arnos Grove still has its bronze ticket hall windows from 1933.

Only one solitary payphone remains at Cockfosters, nestled between the two staircases leading up from the ticket hall.

Northfields shows the effect of the large ticket hall 'box' created by the architect Charles Holden, with dark bricks at ground level and the main box in red brick with a concrete roof. The uplighters and bench are modern.

ROUNDELS

The familiar 'bar-and-circle' device, now known as the roundel, was introduced onto the platforms of London's underground railways from around 1908. This followed some experimentation to make the station names easier to see, particularly on the platforms of the sub-surface lines where it seemed that every spare piece of wall was taken up with a haphazard display of advertisements. The symbol also started to make its appearance outside stations.

The bullseye, as the symbol was originally known, varied considerably in its dimensions, unlike today's carefully controlled logo. However, on the three UERL tube railways it was standardised with a circle diameter of 54 inches. The name plate was surrounded by a wooden frame, and the signs were made by Chromo, of Wolverhampton (below).

The circle was solid red until a ring was introduced in 1917 when the symbol was redrawn by Edward Johnston. It was around this time that guidelines as to the proportions of the bullseye were introduced, although these were not always strictly heeded. It also took well over a decade for the older roundels to be replaced, and there are still a very small number of solid disc roundels to be found on the network. The one at Caledonian Road is original, but those at Ealing Broadway are replicas installed in 1992.

In the 1920s the red ring was given a neat border inside and out. The blue bar had a moulded wooden frame, originally painted red. The design was registered in 1917, as Registered Design 659,814; this number appeared on signs produced until the registration expired in 1932 (below).

Caledonian Road, c.1908

Barons Court, 1920s, showing the registration number in the lower right corner

The first platform name signs to resemble those still used today were designed in 1916. The designs were registered on 19 March 1917, and the registration number 659814 appeared on most signs made until the design registration expired in 1932, after 15 years. The signs were made by a variety of manufacturers, including Chromo of Wolverhampton and Franco Signs of London.

The wholesale replacement of signs at many central area stations in the 1960s led to many of the signs being scrapped and replaced with a simpler style. The more recent station refurbishment programme has resulted in many of the survivors being replaced as well, fortunately by modern replicas. A few still remain on the network, and can be distinguished both by their appearance — they are more worn than modern signs — and sometimes the presence of the maker's name or the registered design number somewhere on the enamelled panels. Unlike the previous signs with solid red discs, the manufacturer's name was not often applied to these signs.

The red rings on the signs are lined in black, with a further thicker black outline around the outside. The most noticeable feature is the 1 inch thick shaped wooden surround for the bar. This was often painted red originally, but in later years blue paint was used. The signs were usually formed of two enamelled sheets with the lower sheet having the blue bar and station name along its top edge.

There are now very few of the original signs left around the network. St James's Park retains several, including one unique version on the eastbound platform that lacks the possessive 's'. It is also unusual in having the blue bar painted onto the upper enamelled sheet. Barons Court has some of its roundels on wide, single sheets, and all have red-painted mouldings. A few exist on the south end of the Northern line, but most were replaced by replicas during refurbishment in the 1990s.

The unique sign at St James's Park which omits the possessive 's'.

The registered number on a sign at St James's Park is just visible, the sign having settled in its frame over the years.

Silhouette roundels at Cockfosters and Uxbridge.

Cockfosters received the first of what were termed 'silhouette' roundels, in which the counters (the white semicircles between the ring and the bar) were omitted, showing the wall behind. These remained the only such type on the system until more recent times, when their popularity has increased.

After the Second World War, some roundels appeared with text in the counters. Usually this was 'London Transport', but at some stations opened just before and after the war the line name appeared, with London Transport across the bar. Most of these roundels have been removed, but one of the former design remains at Aldgate East (see p99).

The 1950s saw the introduction of plainer, unlined roundels. These were usually enamelled onto large square signs with white backgrounds, and appeared at many stations both above and below ground. A variation was introduced in 1968 with the Victoria line, this having the sign formed onto glass and being illuminated from behind. At stations north of King's Cross a cheaper style of sign was used, in which an enamelled roundel was tilted back slightly, and lit from above with a recessed fluorescent tube.

The roundels incorporated into the glazing at Sudbury Town have shortened bars and use a different typeface (see also p103).

A few stations use miniature metal-framed roundels on their trackside walls, such as this example at Highgate, from 1941.

In the early 1970s the proportions of the symbol were changed, and the name 'roundel' was adopted for it. Experiments were made by changing the colours: initially, all-red roundels were trialled at Sloane Square in 1971 and Cannon Street. It was soon realized that the bar bearing the name needed to be in a different colour, and then yellow counters were trialled. It was soon decided that the red ring and blue bar on a white background formed the best symbol for the Underground, although all-red roundels without text were retained for signs outside stations for some years and one remains at Camden Town.

A different type of illuminated roundel was tried on the new Jubilee line stations, opened in 1979. They were again backlit, but were set into a shaped aperture so that only the roundel was lit. They were not successful, and only lasted until 1988.

Station refurbishments from the late 1980s received some different styles of roundel. Mansion House received solid roundels with and without counters when it reopened in 1991 after major redevelopment work. These are made of plastic; the silhouette type had previously been provided at Heathrow Terminal 4 from its opening in 1986.

The only remaining all-red roundel from the early 1970s, above the Kentish Town Road entrance at Camden Town.

The greater standardization of roundels came about with the introduction of the Underground sign manual. Whereas the proportions of the bar and size of the text had been varied according to the length of the station name, the bar was now fixed in size. Double lines of text on roundels can now only be seen at High Street Kensington (below).

The largest roundel on the Underground today is probably that on the entrance to Arsenal station (opposite). It followed a similar solid-disc roundel erected over the Highgate Hill entrance to Archway station (then called Highgate). Canary Wharf has the largest platform roundels ever used, the ring being 158 cm in diameter.

This 1930s style of sign is on a single sheet of enamel, and is at the entrance to Temple station.

The large mosaic roundel outside Arsenal station dates from 1934, when the station was rebuilt with a wider façade.

POINTING THE WAY

From the time the underground railways opened in London there has been a need to direct passengers: to the ticket hall, to the platforms and trains, and to the exits. A number of styles of directional arrow have been used, reflecting the era in which they were put up, the development of LT corporate design, and more recently a more standardized arrow which is perhaps more in keeping with other directional signage, but less characterful than its predecessors.

The Victorian and Edwardian eras favoured pointing hands, often with a small piece of cuff, to direct passengers. Somewhat surprisingly one of these signs has survived at Stepney Green station, painted onto a wall. North Ealing also uses a hand on a solitary direction sign for the westbound platform, though at the time of writing a poorly executed copy was in place.

Stepney Green, probably 1902

Illuminated arrows were used on the train describers installed at Earl's Court and other stations when the MDR was electrified and resignalled in 1905/6 see p101. These arrows have a small flared base. In contrast, the three tube railways opened in the following two years by the UERL featured art deco styling, but with two slightly different designs of arrow used by different tile manufacturers. Those made by Maw & Co. had flared shafts and finely drawn heads (as shown on pages 7-10). The arrows from George Wooliscroft & Son were similar, but with heavier heads and bases. The most common style of arrow on Underground signs (as opposed to tiling) has been that with flights on its tail, known as a Mexican arrow.

The original (above) and replica (below) signs at North Ealing.

Golders Green, probably 1923

Cockfosters

One key feature of the arrows used by London Transport is the juxtaposition with the roundel sign. Like other graphic devices, this evolved over time, before settling down to a consistent form around the mid-1930s. The four-flight arrow shown at Ealing Common places the arrow across the bar of the roundel, whereas the arrow was sometimes split either side of the bar; no examples of this remain today.

Ealing Common, 1931

In the mid-1930s the arrow and roundel were combined into one symbol: an arrow passing through a circle. The arrow passed through a red circle (often lined), when produced on an enamel sign. On illuminated signs the whole of the arrow would be white, but the circle could be either white or red, all on a black background.

The arrows employed by the Underground group from around 1930, which continued under the auspices of the LPTB are perfectly weighted, by contrast to those from earlier years. They can generally be dated by reference to the number of flights, although exceptions to this can be found, and there is some overlap in the time periods for 2- and 3-flight arrows:

- 4 flights: Late 1920s – c.1933; no circle on the shaft
- 3 flights: c.1933 – c.1950
- 2 flights: c.1946 onwards

The final example is the modern arrow, which started to appear in the 1970s. It is a standard design, used by many companies and whilst it is functional it lacks the style and character of the earlier arrows.

Right: Four-flighted arrow at Gloucester Road, three flights at Piccadilly Circus, two at Highgate and none at Chiswick Park.

Below: This 1932 sign at Chiswick Park has a smaller sign beneath highlighting its heritage status.

PICCADILLY
KINGS CROSS
COCKFOSTERS

TRAINS
2/908

HIGHGATE
WAY OUT

CHISWICK PARK
WAY OUT

STATION NAME FRIEZES

Underground passengers take for granted the fact that the station name will be repeated on a strip along the platform just above head height, making station recognition simple. However, it wasn't always like this. Early stations had their name signs lost in a clutter of advertising, and even the smartly tiled stations of the UERL only featured the name three times per platform (see p7–9).

In 1937 the LPTB installed a name frieze along the Northern line platforms at Tottenham Court Road station. It was printed on paper, and the names alternated with coloured, unlettered roundels. The experiment was a success, as within two years new stations had the friezes incorporated into their tiling. Swiss Cottage, St John's Wood, and Baker Street on the new Bakerloo line extension demonstrate this (see photograph on p17). However, the addition of friezes to existing stations progressed very slowly, if at all, during the Second World War; even major station such as Piccadilly Circus had to wait until the end of the war.

With war past, progress began to be made. New tube platforms, such as those on the eastern extensions of the Central line, had their names tiled in the same way as the pre-war Bakerloo stations. Where the friezes were added to existing platforms they were supplied as a series of enamelled plates which were screwed over the tiles. The names and roundels were on separate plates and again alternated along the platform. Unlike the original frieze the roundels were in the line colour, with the line name in capitals across the bar, and the entire frieze had an upper and lower stripe of the line colour. An example of this style of frieze remains at Holland Park (below, left).

The Victoria line stations all had a similar frieze, which differed from those that were on other stations. The lettering was white on a band of Victoria line blue, with blank white roundels between the names. A slightly narrower black band ran above the frieze with 'Way out' and arrows in white above each frieze roundel. Only Pimlico retains these.

The opening of the extension to Heathrow in the 1970s saw a modification of the Victoria line style. The white roundels were retained, but at Heathrow Central the black bands above were narrower, and alternated between 'Way out' and 'Airport' in yellow capitals with arrows. These also included the international pictograms for the two directions. Hatton Cross and the new platforms at Hounslow West feature narrower friezes with the 'Way out' signs interspersed with the name.

The new Jubilee line stations from Baker Street to Charing Cross followed a similar style, but used the station names in black to improve the contrast against the pale grey of the line colour. The colours in the strip above the frieze were reversed from the Heathrow stations as part of the station design in which the platform exits were highlighted by yellow panelling.

The massive station refurbishment programme of the 1980s included a new design of name frieze. Frustrated by the plethora of cables used around stations, which ended up being placed in ugly trunking running over tiles and spoiling the station décor, a new solution was devised. Plastic units using the line colour could be fitted along the platform walls and could contain all the cabling, with room to spare for future services. The station name was carried in white capitals on alternate sections; the other sections continued to show white roundels. A white stripe ran along the frieze and contained the 'Way out' signs. The trunking was not the same style at every station.

Not every station needed the cable trunking, and so where a new or replacement frieze was required a more minimal solution was found. The enamelled plates were retained, but the roundels were omitted and the line colour became a simple strip along the top edge. Some stations on the Circle line received more decorative signs, with coloured roundels and borders.

The chunky plastic cable trunking was only installed for a few years before fashions changed again, and station refurbishment tended to favour the installation of vitreous enamel panelling fitted to frameworks that held them clear of the original tiled walls. The friezes were incorporated into the panelling with just a single stripe of colour above. By the time that these refurbishments were taking place the name was appearing in dark blue New Johnston typeface.

A variation of this type of frieze has since become the standard for use at refurbished stations with tiled walls. It consists of a raised enamelled strip formed as a narrow box-section, bearing the name, coloured stripe, and (where necessary) black 'Way out' patches with direction arrows. At some stations it forms a continuous strip along the platform wall; at some of the UERL stations that retain their original tiling designs the frieze is interrupted so that it does not cut across the integral Way Out signs in the tiling. Other stations with interrupted friezes are those on the sub-surface lines where the platform wall consists of a series of brick arches, and the frieze is installed within the recesses.

At Edgware Road and Mornington Crescent, both stations were closed for refurbishment works. They were retiled in the original UERL style and new cable trunking was placed above the tiling, with down-lighting to illuminate the frieze.

The Jubilee line pioneered a new style of name frieze when its extension from Green Park to Stratford opened in 1999. The frieze is in the same style as the previous enamelled signs, but made of glass, allowing it to be effectively back-lit by fluorescent tubes. As they are not enclosed on their lower edge the lighting illuminates the platform wall as well. This frieze incorporates panels with directions to other lines, lifts, and exits. At Bermondsey station an error was made and the original frieze had white lettering on a dark blue background.

DECORATIVE PANELLING

For almost ninety years, the predominant decoration for tube platforms was tiling. As previous sections have shown, a variety of decorative tiled effects were used over that period. At the end of the 1970s, a new type of decoration was tried: panelling. This was quicker to install, as the panels could be far larger than individual tiles. Complex pictures were easier to produce, without grouting lines cutting across. Although it is possible to create detailed tiled pictures, the tiles are expensive (each typically being unique) and putting them up is necessarily more time-consuming than if they are all the same. The disadvantage of panelling is that a metal framework has to be fitted onto the platform wall, and this reduces the width of the platform slightly.

One of the first panelled stations was Charing Cross. When the Jubilee line was created in 1979, the Bakerloo line station at Trafalgar Square was merged with the Northern line's Strand station, and the platforms were redecorated. Those on the Northern line were given striking black-and-white murals created from woodcuts by the artist David Gentleman, depicting the construction of the original Charing Cross. The Bakerloo line platforms received panels showing pictures from

the nearby National Gallery and National Portrait Gallery, completed in 1981. The Jubilee line platforms were mostly tiled in green, with small panels showing a close-up view of Nelson's statue placed along the platforms.

The panelling was a success, and panelling was chosen as part of the 'kit of parts' for 1980s station refurbishment. The Charing Cross panels were made of melamine; future stations used enamelled metal panels, which were more expensive to produce but gave greater fire resistance. It is probably no coincidence that one of the first to be panelled this way was the northbound Victoria line platform at Oxford Circus, which was extensively damaged by a fire in November 1984.

In 1986, the platforms at Marble Arch were redecorated. They were largely unchanged since they opened in 1900, and it was felt that a station serving one end of London's busy Oxford Street deserved a brighter image. A series of vitreous enamelled panels depicting the Marble Arch in a variety of colours and decorative effects were placed along each platform, with the roundel name signs within each arch. They were designed by the artist Annabel Grey.

Other stations with vitreous enamelled panels include Euston (Northern line, West End branch) and Embankment (both in 1987) and Holborn (1988).

CHARING CROSS
NO SMOKING

← WAY OUT
NO SMOKING
CHARING CROSS
EdWARdE
IIII
ANNA
BOLINA
B
LADI
MARI
HENRY
VIII

MARBLE ARCH
Way out

MARBLE ARCH

MARBLE ARCH
Big and Small

MARBLE ARCH

MARBLE ARCH
RED DOG

ORNAMENTAL METALWORK

South Kensington was rebuilt in 1907 with a new arcade across the cutting in which the platforms reside. Steps led from the arcade to a basement-level ticket hall. The entrances to the arcade from Pelham Street and Thurloe Place received ornate iron grilles showing the name of the station and the companies operating it. Early photographs show the grille to be unpainted (or all painted a dark colour), but in recent years it has had the lettering highlighted in cream, to good effect.

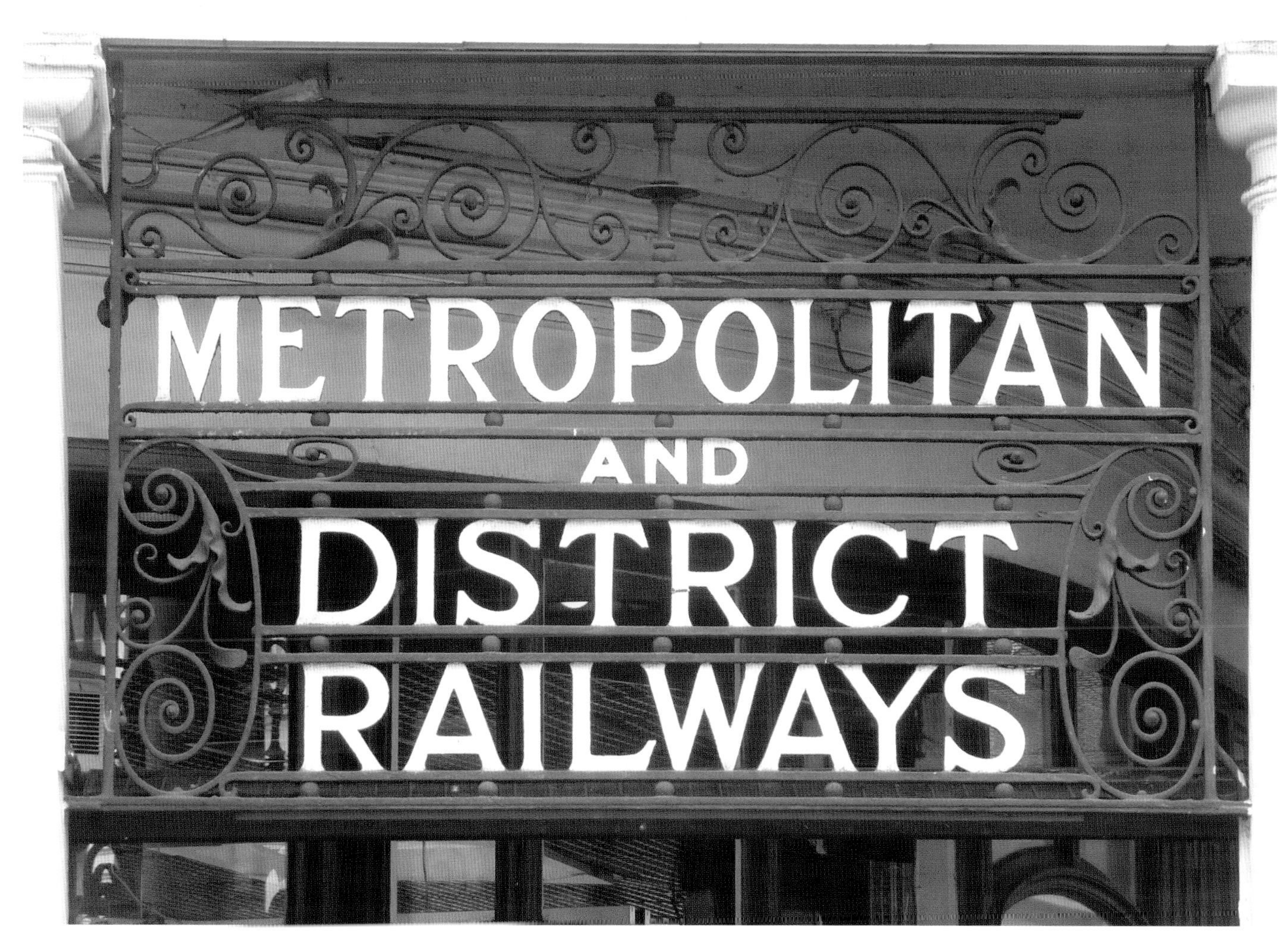

South Kensington, 1907

Edgware Road lift grille, 1907, with the 1992 enlarged replica below.

The tube railways opened by the UERL in 1906-7 had a number of Art Nouveau flourishes applied by the company's architect, Leslie Green. One of these was the provision of decorative grilles above lift shafts and ticket offices. These featured curving, plant-like forms typical of the style. A nice feature at Edgware Road station, on the Bakerloo line, is the installation of a larger replica of a lift grille over the station entrance following station refurbishment work.

Other ironwork at the UERL stations was provided around the stairwells in the street for the small number without surface buildings. Tottenham Court Road was one such station, and had elaborate signs including the fare and travel time to various other stations erected above its stairwells. The signs were progressively modified over the years, with roundels in place of the 'Hampstead Tube' sign, and the stairwells were roofed over for a short period. Rather plain roundel signs are now over the stairwells, but the railings are still original. Very ornate metal railings were erected around the subway entrances at King's Cross station, which gave access to the City & South London Railway. The initials of the company (CSL) were 'woven' into the curlicues of the ironwork.

In 1923 the Hampstead Tube was extended northwards from its terminus at Golders Green to Hendon. A single intermediate station was opened at Brent, on an embankment. The station building was at ground level, and a subway cut through the embankment connecting the ticket hall to the stairs rising to the single island platform. The subway took the form of an arched passage, and a metal grille filled the shape of the elliptic arch at the ticket hall end, above the sliding gates. The ironwork resembles a rising sun; alternatively it could be seen as a metaphor for the Underground, sending rails out from the centre of London in all directions (especially to the north). It is in keeping with the Art Deco style that was beginning to make itself felt in art and architecture at the time.

Tottenham Court Road

Ravenscourt Park

Brent Cross

Chalk Farm

More Art Deco metalwork appeared with the opening of the Piccadilly line extension to Cockfosters. The stations in tunnel, at Manor House, Turnpike Lane, and Wood Green received ornate alloy grilles over the ventilation ducts placed at regular intervals along the platform walls. These were individual to each station, and were designed by Harold Stabler. When Wood Green ticket hall was rebuilt in 1988 to accommodate the new Underground Ticketing System, a metal balustrade was provided along the upper edge of the ticket office, which now projected forward. The balustrade was decorated with metal figures derived from the platform ventilation grilles.

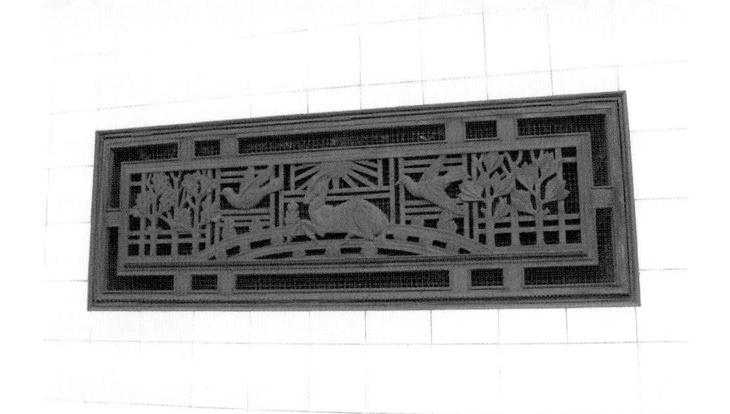

Turnpike Lane (above) and Manor House (below). The grille at Wood Green, together with the ticket hall motifs are shown opposite.

PLATFORM SHELTERS

Most stations have provided some form of shelter for passengers waiting for trains, but the quality of accommodation has varied considerably between railway company and over time. Such diversity is reflected today in the various shelters provided at different stations.

One of the oldest waiting rooms on the Underground today is on the eastbound platform at North Ealing. As the photograph (right) shows, this is a neat wooden building containing a wooden bench seat around the inside. An arched opening leads in, and an ample awning with decorative valance provides additional shelter outside.

Another venerable survivor is on the eastbound platform at East Acton station, which was opened by the GWR in 1920. The Underground had running rights over the line so that their trains could reach Ealing Broadway. The station was a simple affair, with wooden platforms and shelters for passengers. The remaining shelter has a large canopy projecting forwards above the platform, and contains a small waiting room. Like that at North Ealing, the canopy has a decorative valence around its edge. The westbound platform has an even smaller waiting room of slightly different design.

Dating from the early 1930s, Ealing Common station features attractive seating on both platforms near the bottom of the stairs, set back to keep passengers sheltered from wind and rain. Another nearby station redesigned by Charles Holden in the 1930s is Chiswick Park, which features neat glazed enclosures on the platforms ; the same style of shelter was also provided at Stamford Brook (see p79). Glazed draught screens have also been provided at the supports to the concrete canopies, again to provide some shelter to passengers.

During the late 1930s, stations on the Metropolitan line were being rebuilt as part of the works to extend the Bakerloo line northwards to Stanmore. The track rearrangements necessitated the rebuilding of the platforms at West Hampstead, Kilburn, and Dollis Hill. Waiting rooms on the new island platforms were given distinctive curved glass ends with metal glazing bars, and were fully enclosed. The bases of the walls used brick, which was sometimes tiled. Rayners Lane received similar waiting rooms on each platform at around the same time. Work to enlarge Harrow-on-the-Hill station was started as well, but completion was delayed until 1948 because of the Second World War. Each of the three island platforms received similar curved glazing in the waiting rooms at their southern ends. Wembley Park and Finchley Road had more conventional waiting rooms provided on their platforms, but with the same style of metal framed windows on either side.

North Ealing, probably c.1903

East Acton, 1920

Kilburn, 1938

West Acton, 1940

Hainault, 1948

PLATFORM FURNITURE

From the first days of the Metropolitan Railway seats were provided on platforms for waiting passengers to rest upon. Early drawings of Baker Street station show wooden seats fitted in the niches created by the arches along the platform walls. The most common form of seating appeared to be large wooden benches, often displaying the station name clearly along their backs; in many cases this seems to be the only place that the name was displayed on the platform, so pity the poor passenger trying to work out where he was when the benches were occupied! The tube railway companies used lighter benches on their platforms, more akin to garden furniture.

Barons Court, 1905

Another type of seat that has remained popular on the Underground for many years is the simple wooden form that uses the platform wall as its back. This emerged in the 1920s and were installed on the extension of the C&SLR to Morden, opened in 1926. The 1930s Piccadilly line extension to Cockfosters made use of them as well, placed regularly along the wall, as shown on p16, and the 1939 Bakerloo line and Central line extensions used a slatted version of the seats. This style was also used in the Victoria line stations of the 1960s, as can be seen in the photograph of Victoria on p20–21.

Uxbridge, 1938

These sheltered platform seats at Turnham Green probably date back to the reconstruction of the station in 1911.

In 1932 a new platform was opened at Stamford Brook as part of works to rearrange the track layout to accommodate an extension of the Piccadilly line. It has this neat sheltered waiting area with integral seating.

The 1930s saw the rise of the back-to-back bench seats with roundels in the middle, effectively forming a backrest. These were introduced by a number of different railway companies in a variety of styles. The most familiar style still found around the Underground today is that at High Street Kensington shown on page 54. Similar seats with roundels can be seen at Hammersmith, Earl's Court, Arnos Grove, and Harrow-on-the-Hill stations.

When White City station was constructed just after the Second World War, its platform furniture was given more smooth curves through the use of metal pipe frames. The roundels had, uniquely, curved corners on the upper edge of the bar, and some had wooden seats constructed around them. More modern versions of the back-to-back seats can be found at Northfields and Gants Hill, where they incorporate lighting units (see photographs on p49 and p121).

White City, 1947

Some railway companies incorporated their monogrammed initials on as many items of station furniture as they could. The companies that joined together to form the Underground mostly avoided this (although the roundel became fairly ubiquitous). However, some of the stations opened by main-line companies which then became part of the Underground still retain platform seats in which the monograms are placed into the cast-iron end pieces.

Hammersmith (Circle and H&C lines) has two types of GWR bench: this with the art deco symbol, and an earlier style with more ornate lettering.

LTSR bench at Plaistow

Hornchurch is the only Underground station to feature this style of Midland Railway bench. No fewer than seven are still on its platforms.

CANOPIES

The varied ownership of the railways that comprise today's Underground can be seen in part from the brackets that support the canopies protecting travellers from the elements whilst waiting for their train. In Victorian times these cast iron structures tended to be decorative, adding to the attractiveness of the station. To their credit, LU have retained many of them and highlighted them as part of station refurbishment work in recent years. Some of the oldest brackets remaining on stations opened by Underground railway companies (as opposed to main-line stations subsequently taken over) are found on the Hammersmith & City and Metropolitan lines.

The Metropolitan Railway stations opened in 1889 and 1892 were given very ornate brackets which remain in good condition today. Most of the 1889 canopies have at least one conjoined bracket, as shown above. The rather plain brackets at Willesden Green probably date from the station rebuilding in 1925, and are also to be seen at Aldgate.

Also worth recording here are the ornate column capitals at the 1889 stations; they can just be seen below the canopy brackets in the photograph of Chalfont & Latimer (below, left).

Amersham, 1892

Westbourne Park, probably 1870s

Chalfont & Latimer, 1889

Willesden Green, 1925

The examples on this page and the next two are all from stations on the Central line which were originally opened by the Eastern Counties Railway (ECR), which opened as far north as Loughton in 1856. The brackets with the curved design, pictured at Leyton, come in two forms: a smaller bracket which was paired on columns, and a larger, wall-mounted bracket. Both types can be seen in the picture at Leyton. South Woodford features two other styles, and has three different types of bracket. This might be the result of the station being reconstructed in 1883. Its neighbour to the north, Woodford (page 85), has a unique style of bracket which is rather more ornate that the other ECR stations. However, all of these brackets are distinctive through their use of abstract, mostly geometric designs.

Although the ECR promoted the northward extension of the line from Loughton to Epping and Ongar, it had been taken over by the Great Eastern Railway by the time this extension was constructed. Theydon Bois station has brackets featuring a GER monogram. A different style of monogram bracket was used on the 1903 line from Woodford through to Hainault and beyond.

Leyton, 1856

Snaresbrook, 1856

South Woodford, showing the other two styles

A GER monogram bracket from Hainault, 1903.

The ornate style of bracket unique to Woodford.

This page and the next feature a variety of brackets from stations opened by main line companies. Of particular interest is the selection on display at Plaistow: like South Woodford, three different styles are in use. This might result from the partial rebuilding in 1905, creating the bay platform, as it is the brackets alongside which differ from the more standard 'LTSR' monograms, shown far right.

Kew Gardens, opened by the LSWR

Harrow & Wealdstone, opened by the LNWR.

Wimbledon Park, opened by the LSWR.

Plaistow (above and below), opened by the LTSR.

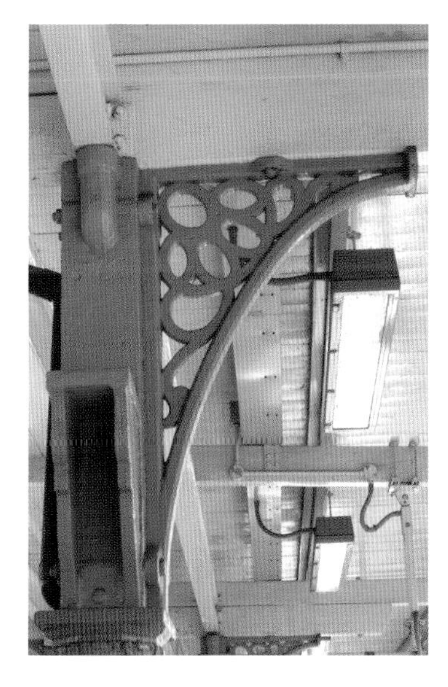

East Ham, with LTSR monogram brackets

High Barnet, opened by the GNR.

One feature common to most of the older Underground stations with platforms outside is the wooden canopy with its decorative edging (known as a valance). Different companies seemed to favour different styles of edging; presumably it was a subtle way of being distinctive. No attempt is made here to categorize the different designs still to found around the network, but instead a selection is shown to indicate the variety

Barkingside, opened by the Great Eastern Railway.The same design is also found at Newbury Park, Fairlop, Hainault, Grange Hill, Chigwell, Snaresbrook, South Woodford, and Buckhurst Hill stations.

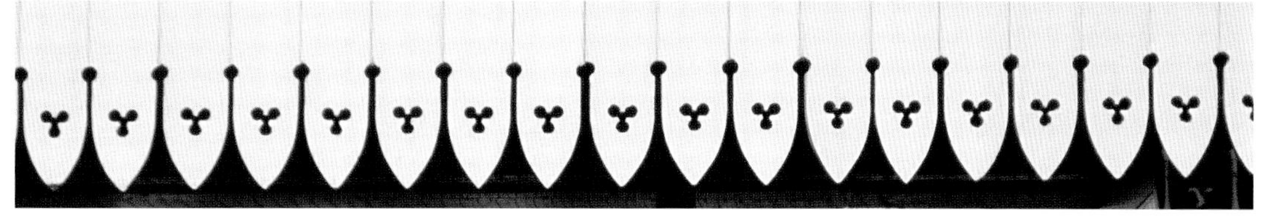

Woodford has an unusually ornate valance, but it is only on part of the canopy, the rest being plain.

This stepped style of valance, seen here at South Kensington, is also used at High Street Kensington. Until their redevelopment c.1990, the platforms at Gloucester Road also used this style of valance.

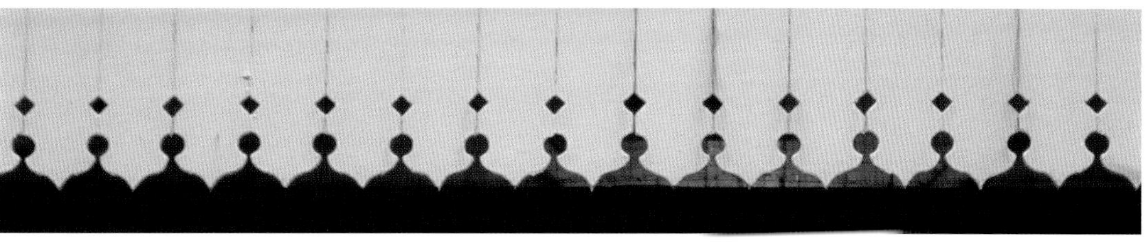

Chorleywood (seen left), Chesham, and Pinner have the same style. Chalfont & Latimer used to be the same, but the decorative points along much of the main edge have been removed at some time in the past.

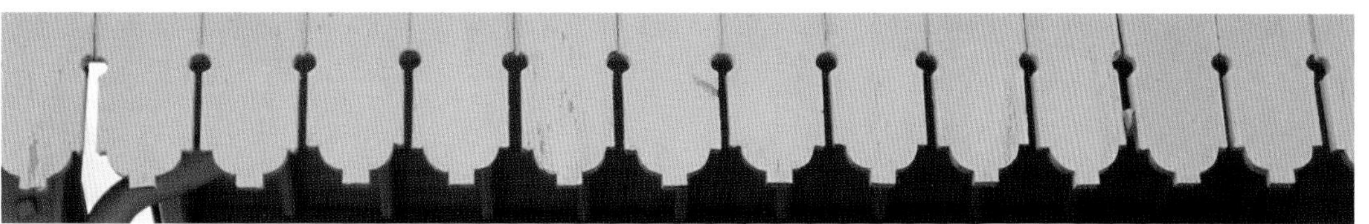

Amersham differs in style from its neighbouring stations, presumably because the line on from Chalfont & Latimer was built slightly later.

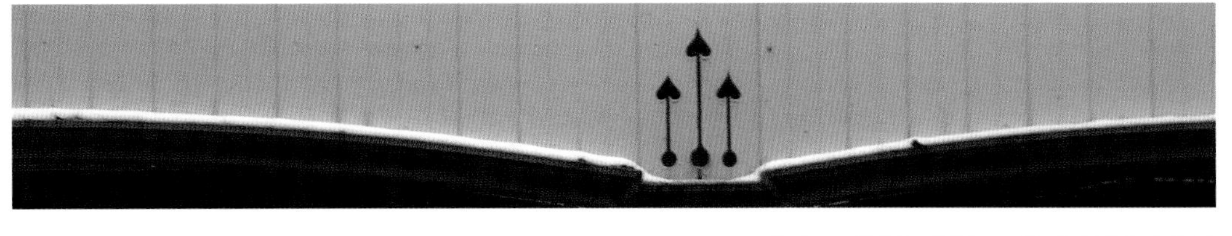

The Metropolitan line platforms at Baker Street have sections of canopy formed as long arches with decorative cut-outs and a painted lower edge.

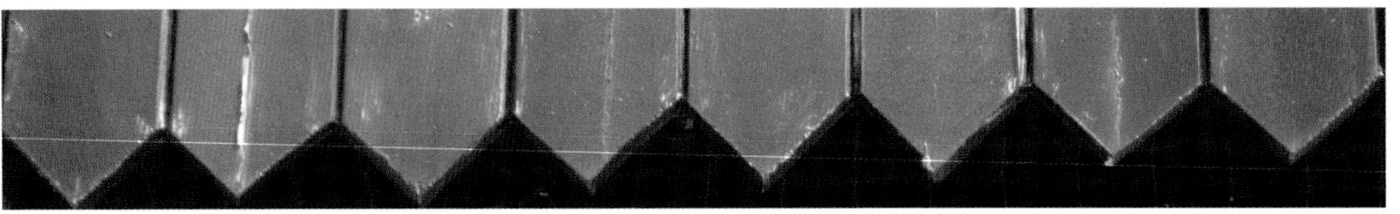

A simple saw tooth profile is used on the canopies at Northwick Park. The same design (but painted white) can also be found at Edgware Road and on a section of canopy at South Woodford.

Hammersmith (left) and Ladbroke Grove, both on the Circle and Hammersmith & City lines, have the same style of valance.

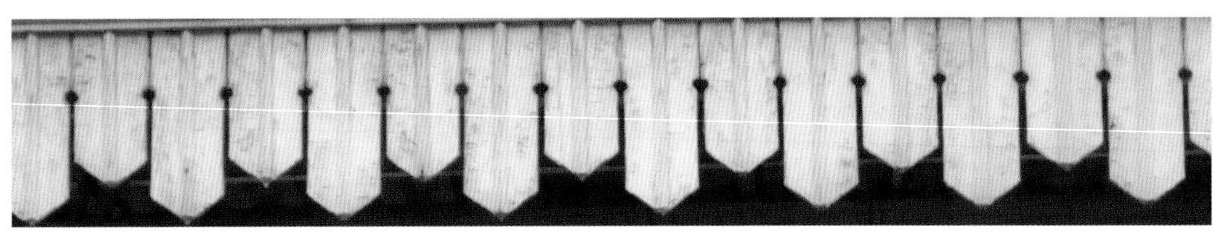

Westbourne Park is a rare example of valance boards alternating in length.

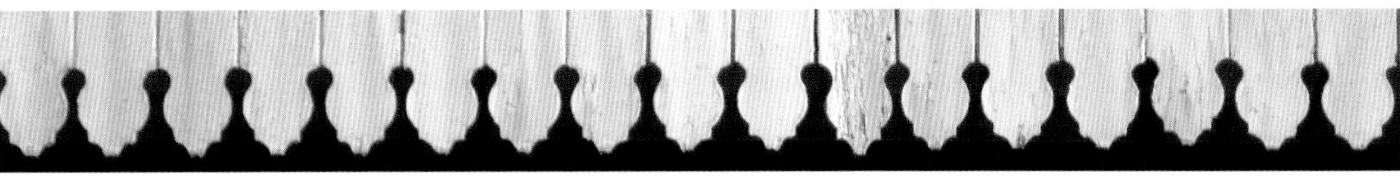

Latimer Road is another station with a unique design of valance. It has been repainted since this photo was taken as part of station refurbishment work.

Turnham Green (left), Stamford Brook, and Ravenscourt Park all have the same style of valance. The horizontal beading across the valance is painted yellow at Ravenscourt Park.

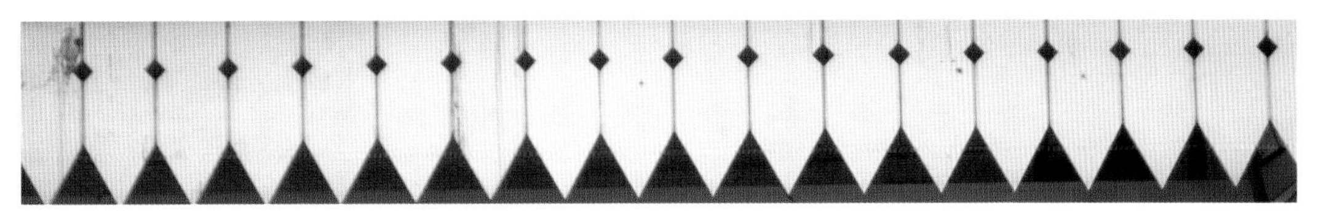

The design at West Kensington is similar to that at Hammersmith and Ladbroke Grove, but with more sharply pointed 'teeth' along the edge.

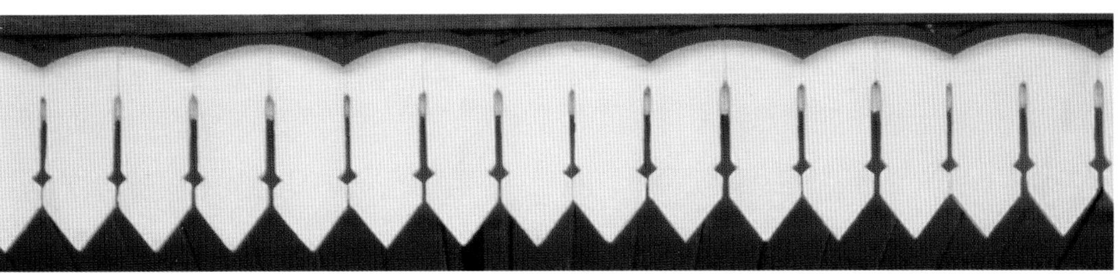

The Great Northern Railway stations at High Barnet, Totteridge & Whetstone (left) and Woodside Park have a similar design to that above, but with wider slots above the diamond shaped hole. Early photographs show the slots to be of a consistent width; perhaps repeated painting has led to the irregular look shown here.

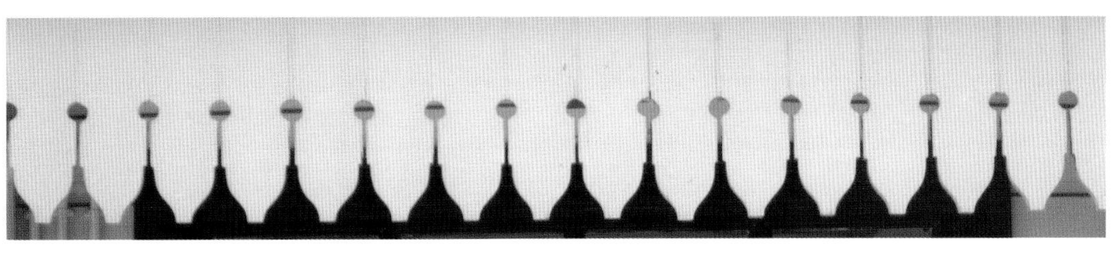

The stations opened by the LSWR at Southfields (left) and Wimbledon Park both share this design of valance, although that at Wimbledon Park is painted the more conventional white.

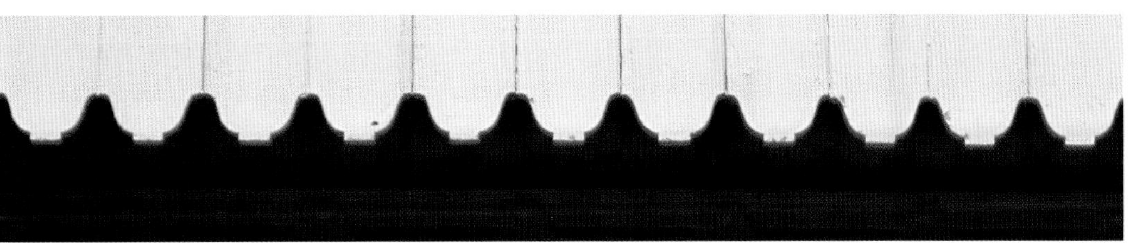

Willesden Junction has a similar valance style to that at Kenton (left), but with greater vertical exaggeration of the features.

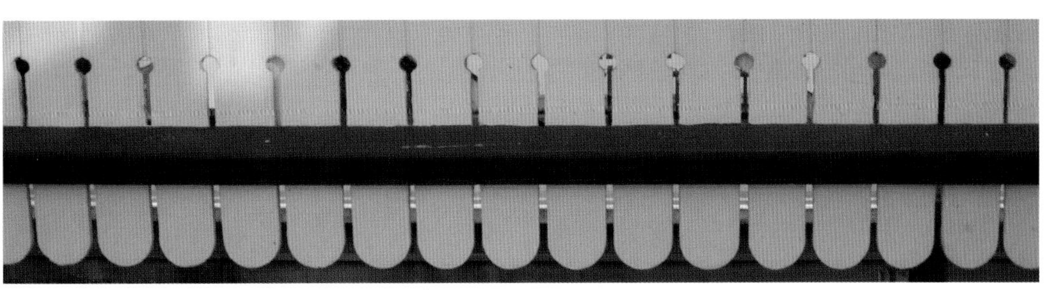

North Ealing has a valance with a distinctive 'tongue' shape to the boards. The same design is used on the small waiting room on the eastbound platform, shown on p74.

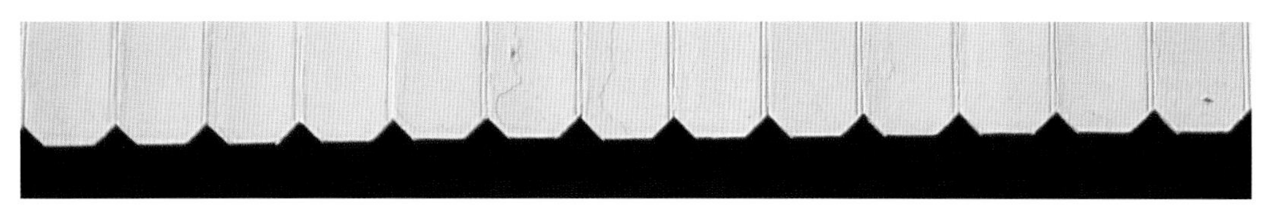

Neasden (left) and Willesden Green share this simple design of valance. That at Ruislip is similar, but with deeper notches and horizontal beading similar to North Ealing.

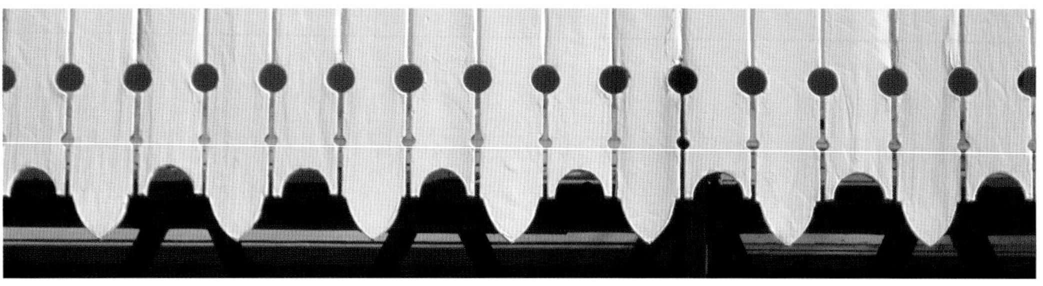

The stations at Plaistow (left), East Ham, and Upton Park all share this elaborate valance design.

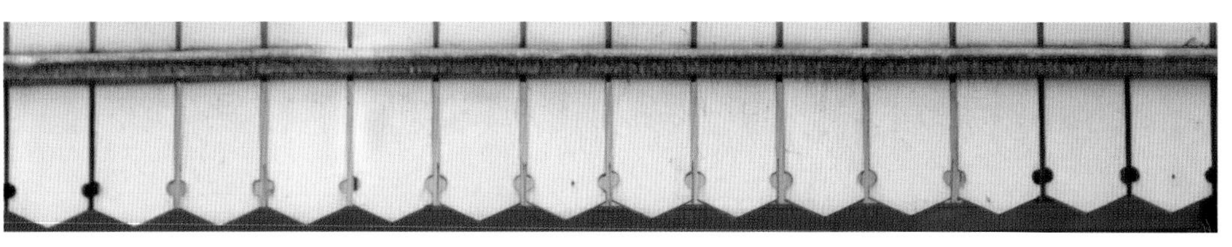

Both Bow Road (left) and Whitechapel share this style of valance, with a simple saw-tooth edge made more interesting with large notches and a line of beading (the latter omitted at Whitechapel). This probably dates from the opening of the Whitechapel & Bow Railway in 1902.

Golders Green is the only station with this style of valance, which is also the only valance to have been used on the Hampstead Tube (all other stations were underground). The style was retained and used on the fifth platform face when this was added in 1923.

The valance at East Acton is only on the former GWR waiting room on the eastbound platform. It has been well-maintained, and the beading is painted to match the window frames and other features of the building.

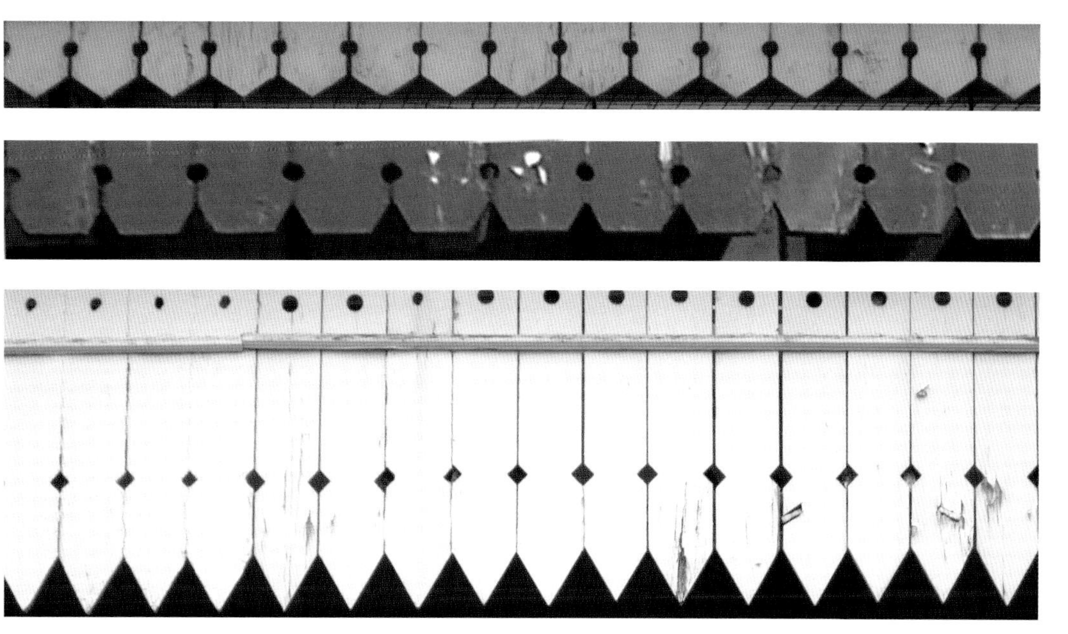

North Acton has a very thin valance—the full height is shown in the photograph—but it closely resembles its neighbour at East Acton.

The canopy at Shoreditch, along with the rest of the station, was removed when the station was closed in 2007. Much of the site of the station is now buried deep under the Overground line.

Boston Manor appears at first glance to be similar to West Kensington. However, it has a line of beading, and an unusual line of extra holes at the very top of each board. The diamond holes clearly show where the boards have become misaligned over time.

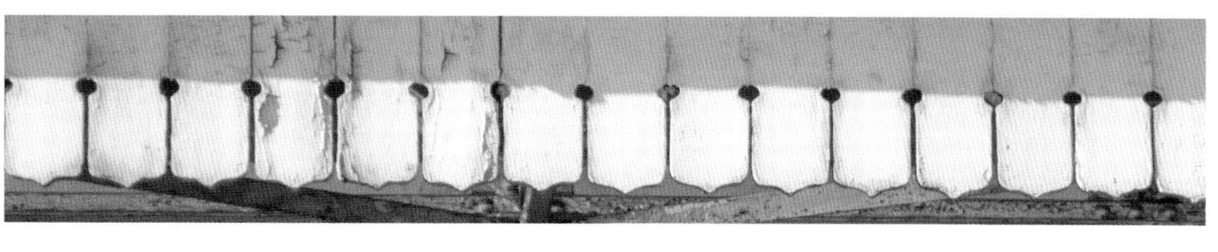

The valance at Barons Court has seen better days. The curved corners and slight points contrast with the sharp points on its neighbour at West Kensington.

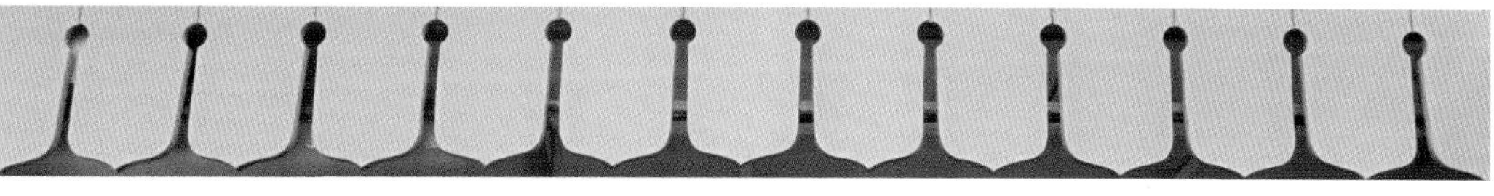

Although their history and locations have nothing in common, the canopy valances at Finchley Central and Mill Hill East (left) are similar to those at Barons Court. The valance at Finchley Central is painted a more conventional white.

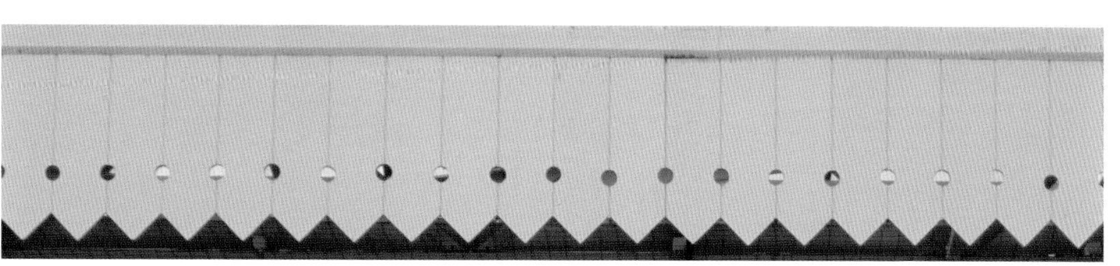

Putney Bridge has a simple sawtooth profile with a 90° point, large holes between the boards, and a line of beading above.

SIGNAGE

There is quite a diversity of heritage platform number signs around the Underground system. Many refurbished stations use the modern standard sign, giving the line name and platform number in blue on a white background with a stripe of colour for the line along the top edge. It is good to see a number of survivors from earlier periods remaining though, often at stations that retain a number of heritage features. A selection is shown on this page.

Rayners Lane, 1938

Cockfosters, 1933

Aldgate, 1930s

Uxbridge, 1938

Northfields, 1932

Putney Bridge has kept this style of platform number sign on platforms 2 and 3.

Holland Park is one of the most unaltered Central London Railway stations, and still has a number of non-standard signs. The 'No Exit' signs at platform level are not in the usual Johnston typeface, suggesting that they date back to the early 1900s.

UNDERGROUND
WARWICK
AVENUE
STATION

A new station building at Shepherd's Bush station on the Central line retains these poster stands from c.1930 outside. They are used to give a history of the station, which is a nice touch.

Reproduction of original 1938 illuminated sign on the forecourt of Uxbridge station.

This trackside sign at Maida Vale has been amended to reflect the change in station names at Charing Cross and Embankment.

Holland Park retains this trackside destination sign from the 1940s, when the line was extended to West Ruislip. It is one of the few remaining signs to show the 'For Ickenham' suffix for the latter station.

The green background to the sign above reflects the use of the colour for both lines when the new Aldgate East station was opened in 1938.

The roundel (below) at the station entrance stairwell is also original, and one of the few remaining with the London Transport name on the counters and the decorative lines above and below UNDERGROUND.

Great Portland Street, 1930s

The 1905 train describer at Earl's Court shows the destination by means of an illuminated arrow. The plates bearing the station names were replaced in 2010, and are not quite in the same style as the originals.

CITY AND
WEST END
TRAINS
BOOKING OFFICE
AND WAY OUT TO
HARROW ROAD FOR
BUSES

Both pages: Sudbury Town uses the unusual seriffed version of the Johnston typeface, designed by Percy Delf-Smith.

CLOCKS

Some of the earliest clocks still to be found on the Underground are those supplied by the Self-Winding Clock Company (SWCC) of New York. Like much of the equipment of the UERL they were American made, and approximately 600 were supplied to the Bakerloo, Piccadilly, and Hampstead Tubes. The company dated back to 1886, after Henry Chester Pond patented the self-winding mechanism two years before. The clock mechanisms were initially made by two other companies with the self-winding mechanism added subsequently, but by the mid-1890s the demand for the clocks was so great that the company had opened its own factory to make the clock mechanisms as well.

The clocks are powered by springs, but save the effort of staff climbing ladders to wind them by using electromagnets. A solenoid mechanism, similar to that found on an electric alarm bell, wound the spring via a ratchet when power was applied. This was triggered by electrical contacts which connected when the main spring was running down, with the electricity coming from two-volt batteries. It would appear that Self-Winding Clocks could use voltages between about 1.5 and 3 volts, allowing modern batteries to be used in original clocks today. An alternative arrangement rewound the spring hourly - by using a smaller portion of the spring greater accuracy was obtained.

The other innovation was the remote synchronization of the clocks. This time Pond was not the inventor, but instead he purchased the patent. An electric pulse sent 30 seconds either side of the hour would bring the minute hand up to the top of the dial. This condition prevented spurious pulses on the line from affecting the clocks.

The only manual intervention needed (apart from occasional battery replacement) was winding each clock on one hour at the start of British Summer Time. In the autumn, synchronizing pulses were sent every minute for an hour, thus retarding the clocks by one hour.

Stations were provided with clocks on their platforms, generally in handsome enamelled copper cases and supported by wrought-iron brackets. These needed to be robust, as vibration and air movement (both common on tube platforms) could otherwise stop the pendulum. The clocks have 24-inch diameter faces on both sides. Ticket hall clocks with 14-inch diameter faces were sometimes fitted in mahogany or oak cases (see photographs of Ravenscourt Park and Maida Vale, right), or suspended from wrought iron brackets.

The clocks continued to be installed as the Underground expanded. On the Bakerloo line extension to Queen's Park the three tube stations north of Paddington had SWCC clocks installed in wooden cases that formed part of the platform-level telephone boxes placed at the end of the lower escalator concourses, as shown in the photograph opposite. These are still in place at Warwick Avenue and Kilburn Park.

This magnificent Self-Winding Clock overlooks the District line platforms at Earl's Court.

When the C&SLR was extended south to Morden in 1926 a new design of mahogany casing was used for the ticket hall clocks in the form of the roundel device (see photograph on p111). Like the clocks, the new cases were all made in the USA. The same style of clock was installed at Ealing Common, since it was rebuilt at around the same time. Other locations may also have received them too; certainly another appears to have been fitted in the ticket hall at Charing Cross station (now Embankment) by 1929. The last new Self-Winding clock on the Underground was installed at Edgware in the early 1930s, possibly as part of work to replace the original clocks on the 1923/4 extension of the Hampstead Tube by Holden's 'roundel' design.

One of the problems with the clocks is that the pair of wires supplying the synchronizing pulse only transmits current for 3 seconds each hour. Telephone engineers, ever on the lookout for spare cables for connecting new equipment, usually assume the cables to be redundant and reuse them for other station systems. The result is that the clocks then lose their synchronization and start to drift.

Ravenscourt Park (left) and Maida Vale

Kilburn Park, 1915

The dials on the clocks were altered to reflect changing trends in clock faces, with the original Roman numerals on some of them being replaced by plain 'tick' marks in the 1930s. Some of the clocks that were changed then changed back after the Second World War, before the plainer design returned to fashion again in the 1960s. Not all clocks were repainted, as can be seen by the manufacturer's name remaining on the faces of some that are still *in situ*. Hampstead, Acton Town, and Russell Square are some of the very small number of stations that retain these clocks without numerals on the face.

Whilst the UERL stations consistently used the Self-Winding Clocks, the other railways forming the Underground chose different suppliers. The CLR used clocks from the Standard Time Company; like the Self-Winding Clocks, these used elaborate wrought-iron brackets to secure them to the walls of the platforms above head height. They were fitted into thick mahogany cases with brass rims, and can still be found at Lancaster Gate, Queensway, and Holland Park stations.

Magneta clocks, made by a Swiss company of that name, were installed across the Metropolitan Railway's stations in the early years of the 20th century. Like the CLR clocks, most of these have long-since been removed, but there are a few survivors. The most obvious sits atop the long 'gateway' between the Metropolitan and Circle line platforms at Baker Street, and still includes the Magneta name on its face. A less obvious example, with a slightly different face is on platforms 3 and 4 at the same station, and others can be found one stop along the Circle line at Edgware Road and also at Liverpool Street.

Some of the stations on the Piccadilly line extensions of the 1930s were fitted with distinctive clocks that used white hands on a blue background, with a simple white edge incorporating the minute marks. Sudbury Town even featured a matching barometer in its ticket hall. At the other end of the Piccadilly line, square clocks were provided in the platform head- and tailwalls. An example of one of these remains at Wood Green.

Harrow-on-the-Hill was rebuilt in the 1940s. After completion each platform was given a large clock suspended from the platform canopy. These remain in use today, and have a very minimal appearance, with simple tick marks at the hours and very slightly tapering hands. The same style of clock was also used at East Finchley, Leytonstone, and White City, and they remain in use at these stations.

Lancaster Gate, 1900

Baker Street, probably c.1925

Edgware Road (Circle, H&C, and District lines), 1926

Turnpike Lane, 1932

The Underground and its predecessors have often used their distinctive logos in a variety of places. Clocks are no exception, as the examples here show. The first example dates to 1925, and features the bar and diamond logo of the Metropolitan Railway. This was a feature of Willesden Green station from its reconstruction by the company's architect, C. W. Clark. The clock face and mechanism has been replaced subsequently. Similar clocks were used at other reconstructed MR stations.

The four underground stations opened on the eastern extension of the Central line in the 1940s featured very distinctive clocks, as illustrated by the example from Gants Hill (below right). The hours were marked by roundels, and a thirteenth roundel was formed using the hour hand. The clocks appear slightly muted because of the blue and black colour scheme, but this increased their visibility. The clock above was changed during refurbishment to have red and blue roundels, but those at Redbridge and Wanstead remain in original colours. The clock at Bethnal Green was refurbished in 2009, and has a beautifully polished brass case, brass hands, and brass rings on the hour roundels. These clocks were made by the Magneta Time Company Ltd.

The final example was installed at Hammersmith station on the District and Piccadilly lines after reconstruction in 1994. It cleverly uses the line colours from the Underground map, with interchange rings at the 3, 6, 9, and 12 o'clock positions, and station tick marks for the other numbers. The hands are a distinctive red. Overall, the clock cleverly integrates into its environment, is clear to read from a distance, and demonstrates a continuation of the practice of re-using Underground symbols for different purposes around the system.

Willesden Green, 1925

Gants Hill, 1947

A unique clock on the Underground was installed shortly after the reconstruction of Piccadilly Circus in the late 1920s. The World Time Clock shows the time across the surface of the Earth through means of a moving band across a Mercator projection map. The band, which moves along a horizontal space representing the equator, marks the time using both 12- and 24-hour notation (using Roman and Arabic numerals respectively). Half of the band is transparent with black numerals, the other half representing night, reverses this.

The clock is set in a bronze case, beneath a glass sign reading "THE WORLD TIME TODAY". It was constructed by the Underground's engineers in the Signal Department workshops. As 'the hub of the Empire', the first plan was to install a bank of clocks in the ticket hall to show the time at key points across the world, but the clock as installed was felt to be a more interesting way of showing the same information (and more).

The band bearing the numerals moves slowly from east to west, and was originally driven by a hand-wound clockwork mechanism. This was replaced by the movement from a Self-Winding clock in 1993, modified to generate the one-second pulses necessary to drive the mechanism by fitting modern opto-electronics that detect the movement of the pendulum.

The map is illuminated from above, being tilted slightly backwards in its case as can be seen in the 1931 photograph (right). The band is backlit (nowadays by fluorescent tubes), and has small vertical arrows pointing from five cities to the time band, enabling the time to be more easily read. These cities are illuminated as points of light on the map, and are London, New York, San Francisco, Cape Town, and Canberra. An additional arrow from London shows British Summer Time.

The World Time Clock fell into disuse around the 1970s. It was refurbished as part of the station refurbishment in the mid-1980s, and restored to working condition in May 1989. It can be found between subways 1 and 4.

The World Time Clock above, and below, a closer look at the moving time band, showing the day/night transition point.

Uxbridge combines a clock with the train destination and 'first train out' indicator board.

Hounslow West is one of the few stations to have kept its 1920s clock with a roundel-shaped wooden case.

PASSIMETERS

The word 'Passimeter' was coined in the USA to describe a ticket booth that could both issue tickets and manage the entrance or exit of passengers, whilst metering (or counting) the flow. They allowed a reduction in station staff, because the same person could sell a ticket, then cancel it and admit entry into the station. Previously the ticket seller and ticket inspector were separate roles. The first passimeter was introduced to the Underground on 16 December 1921 at Kilburn Park station, a clumsy-looking box containing racks of tickets, the punch for cancelling issued tickets, cash machines, and the turnstile mechanism.

Passimeters rapidly proved their worth, as they could issue, date, and cancel 1,000 tickets each hour, and other stations around the system soon acquired them, including Trafalgar Square, Wood Lane, Liverpool Street, and Earl's Court. Instead of the white-painted structures seemingly dotted with windows placed at random, as provided at Kilburn Park, these passimeters were rather more handsome boxes constructed from oak, and with a consistent and more pleasing layout of features. A small row of windows ran above the main windows, some of which opened to provide ventilation for the staff inside. They were typically 10 feet long by 6 feet wide.

Sudbury Town (above), Cockfosters (right), Hounslow West (opposite)

The stations on the Edgware extension of the Hampstead Tube were provided with the same style of passimeter from the outset, although these were made from polished teak. So too were the passimeters at the new stations on the southward extension of the C&SLR to Morden. By the end of 1926 around 43 stations had been equipped with them.

The Central London Railway stations at Bank and Shepherd's Bush had passimeters of a slightly different style. Rather than appearing as wooden structures placed into the booking hall, these looked like they were built in, with tiling on the sides up to the height of the windows. An additional feature at Shepherd's Bush was the provision of a special lane for passengers already holding tickets, who just needed to have them inspected.

Passimeters continued to be installed where stations were rebuilt. London Bridge, Waterloo, Angel, Claphams North and Common, and Kentish Town all benefited from such works. Other major stations with a large passenger traffic were also modified to have multiple passimeters, so that a varying number of queues could be handled depending on demand; Holborn, Bond Street, and Tottenham Court Road stations are examples of this.

Assistance
Zone 4

Piccadilly Circus was rebuilt in 1928, and its new ticket hall was provided with several passimeters. The standard oak passimeter would not have fitted in well with the bronze and marble finishes in the new ticket hall, and so a new design was provided with a bronze frame and marble finishes below the windows. This design was used at many of the stations rebuilt in the early 1930s where similar materials were used. These passimeters had small roundels on their sides, showing the station name. The marble passimeters were designed, like most of the other station fittings, by the station architect, Charles Holden. This was at the request of Frank Pick, who wanted the stations to be carefully designed and appear consistent throughout.

Arnos Grove was built with a large cylindrical ticket hall, and to maintain the symmetry a unique circular passimeter was provided around the central column. Southgate was also cylindrical, but was given a conventional passimeter underneath the column. Both remain *in situ* today, but their use for ticketing has been supplanted by new ticket office at the edges of their respective ticket halls. At Southgate it is used by staff manning the gateline, and the small circular roof above the passimeter has been replaced by a larger roof resembling a squat hat. The lower panels have lost their marble effect, and are now simply painted white.

At Arnos Grove the passimeter was restored in 1990 from its disused condition and now contains displays about the station history. Between November 2006 and March 2007, as part of the Piccadilly line centenary celebrations, it was converted into a studio. The artists Simon and Tom Bloor used it to research the history of the line.

With the advent of Automatic Fare Collection experiments in the 1960s, a new, more modern-looking passimeter was installed at Turnham Green station. This featured larger windows and cleaner lines and was subsequently adopted for use at new Victoria line stations.

Southgate (opposite)

It was the adoption of the Underground Ticketing System in the 1980s that eliminated the long-lasting passimeter. Ticket offices at the sides of the ticket hall, set behind solid walls and toughened glass were more secure, and space was needed in the ticket halls for rows of automatic ticket gates. A series of armed robberies in the early 1980s led to bulletproof glass being installed in the passimeters, but by 1983 the writing was on the wall for the 101 found across the network, and by the end of 1989 tickets were being sold from new ticket offices.

Arnos Grove

LIGHTING

Unlike many Metropolitan Railway stations, the platforms at Croxley have always been electrically lit. These are the original lamp standards, but with replacement lamps and shades.

The lamp brackets outside Queensway are either original from its opening in 1900, or very good replicas.

The red-glazed UERL stations designed by Leslie Green were equipped with hexagonal opal-glass lamps suspended from iron brackets. This is at Gloucester Road.

The UERL also owned the District Railway, and so the hexagonal glass shades were used at some of that company's stations. Barons Court also retains this District Railway monogram on its façade.

The hexagonal shades were used at Kilburn Park (above) and Maida Vale on the 1915 extension of the Bakerloo line.

CHANDELIERS

The extension of the City & South London Railway southwards to Morden, opened in 1926, added seven new stations to the Underground. The buildings were all the work of the architect Charles Holden, and were built from white Portland stone with large windows above the entrances to let light into the ticket halls. Light was very important to Frank Pick, the Managing Director of the Underground: at night, the stations had searchlights on their roofs to show people where they were, and the exteriors were floodlit to highlight the station to people in the street. It was also felt important to illuminate the station interior properly, and one feature designed to help with this was the chandelier.

Wrought iron was used to create the chandeliers. Circular in form, they were suspended from the ceilings by six metal chains spaced equally. Each section of the chandelier between adjacent chains comprised a simple motif of intersecting metal semicircles, and supported four lamps that hung underneath. It is not clear who designed them (although it is known that Holden was not responsible for station fittings), but presumably Pick's aesthetics would only have permitted a light fitting that was both elegant and fit for purpose.

The chandeliers remain today at all the stations with the exception of Tooting Broadway; it is not known when this latter chandelier was removed. They have been fitted with modern energy-saving lamps, and some are protected from roosting pigeons by bird netting, but they are still serving their original purpose of stylish illumination.

Colliers Wood

The heptagonal booking hall at Hounslow West has a chandelier to match, which creates a wonderful shadow pattern on the stepped vault of the ceiling.

UPLIGHTERS

Along with the escalator uplighters (see p122), some of Charles Holden's new Piccadilly line stations had uplit concourses and ticket halls. Piccadilly Circus was the first, following its reconstruction with a subsurface ticket hall and escalators in 1928.

Like those on the escalators, the uplighters on the lower escalator concourses were made of bronze with fluted columns, which tapered slightly towards the small square plinths at the base. The lamp was fitted in a wide, shallow bronze dish, which had curved, stepped, plaster inserts to diffuse the light outwards. The press at the time referred to them as 'fountains of light'. Southgate, Bounds Green, Turnpike Lane, and Piccadilly Circus were all provided with uplighters in this style. Those at the latter station were removed, probably in the 1950s.

Turnpike Lane also received uplighters in its ticket hall. The bronze elements were the same as the previously described lights, but in place of the plaster cone there were opal glass globes within the bronze dishes. The globes were short-lived: photographs show that they had been removed by 1934, and the uplighters have since remained without any feature in the dishes. Bounds Green has had a replica uplighter installed in its ticket hall (there was not one originally), and one of its lower concourse uplighters is also a modern reproduction.

At the other end of the Piccadilly line, the first of Holden's brick and concrete stations at Sudbury Town was provided with uplighters built into the top of two poster stands. They were ugly and incurred the disfavour of Frank Pick, who described them as "illuminated tombstones". The lights, as well as the poster stands, were soon replaced by a pair of tapered uplighters of square cross-section. These were fitted with 500 watt projector lamps to shine upwards, as well as smaller lights shining downwards from the darker 'collar' at the top of the main column. They graduated in colour from yellow to white, with green ornamental bands.

The adjacent station at Sudbury Hill was also rebuilt in the 1930s, in a similar style to its neighbour. The ticket hall was illuminated with a fourth style of uplighter. This had a slender, tapered column rising from a flat square plinth, with a large square dish on top housing the lamp.

Unfortunately both stations at Sudbury had their ticket hall uplighters removed many years ago. Both ticket halls remain uplit, but from modern floodlighting units installed around the edge of the building.

Uplighters have also been added to stations where they were not an original feature. Northfields originally had banks of ticket machines and a Passimeter ticket booth, with the ticket hall lit from floodlights on the Passimeter roof. All of this has been swept away, and the ticket hall now contains four large uplighters installed as part of two bench seats. The same style of lamp, albeit with different seating units, has been provided in the 'Moscow' concourse at Gants Hill since 1996, and are rather more appropriate to the setting than the fluorescent lights originally fitted. A single uplighter of the same type can also be found in the centre of the circular ticket hall at Hanger Lane, surrounded by a seat.

Left: Turnpike Lane, 1932.

Right: The uplighters at Gants Hill are not original to the station, but are well-matched to the large vaulted concourse. They also provide additional seating in an area that previously felt rather empty.

ESCALATOR LIGHTING

The first escalator opened on the Underground in 1911, linking the Piccadilly and District line platforms at Earl's Court. Conventional incandescent lighting was provided as pairs of lamps at regular intervals along the ceiling vault.

Installations of escalators continued to use incandescent lighting for the next sixteen years. However, when Piccadilly Circus station was rebuilt something rather different was provided: uplighting. The balustrades between the escalators were fitted with lines of lights in bronze bowls, standing on fluted bronze columns, shining upwards at the ceiling vault. The effect that this produced was a soft, indirect light unlike anything used previously on the Underground.

This set the standard for the installations of the 1930s, and further uplighters were installed on the new escalators at Highgate (now Archway), Hyde Park Corner, and Marble Arch, all of which were replacing lifts. This was a new family of escalators, manufactured by Otis, and designated as the M-series. The uplighters were made by the General Electric Company.

The extension of the Piccadilly line northwards from Finsbury Park in the early 1930s led to thirteen new escalators being installed at five stations. All were fitted with uplighters and bronze finishes. Further lift-replacement schemes led to uplit escalators being installed at Kentish Town, Holborn, Green Park, Warren Street, Knightsbridge, Chancery Lane, Leicester Square, Earl's Court (Exhibition Centre subway), St Paul's, Swiss Cottage, and St John's Wood.

And that was it. With the start of the Second World War, the reign of the uplighter was over. The new stations on the Central line extension eastwards all used the new fluorescent lighting on their escalators, and a programme of work began to replace incandescent lighting across the system. Regrettably this work included stripping the elegant uplighters from escalators, and replacing them by a bland stripe of fluorescent tubes running down the escalator shaft ceilings. Different styles were used: one was based on the platform lighting, with the tubes held away from the ceiling on supports, whilst another used a continuous strip of light fittings with a curved profile. More recently, diffusers have been used over the tubes.

St John's Wood, 1939

Fortunately the uplighters survived at four stations. Southgate, Swiss Cottage, St John's Wood, and Earl's Court all retained them, although the latter are now in a disused area out of public gaze. The bronze finish has been retained, even after modernization to remove the original wooden treads on the steps.

Southgate

A number of stations have received modern uplighters in brushed stainless steel since the loss of their original lights. This view is of Turnpike Lane.

HOLDEN'S LIGHTING

The stations designed by Charles Holden for the 1930s Piccadilly line extensions, and then other parts of the 1935/40 New Works Programme are characterized by their use of brick and concrete. At the direction of Frank Pick, Holden also designed much of the station furniture to ensure that the stations retained coherent designs. One of the most important areas affected by this decision was the provision of the platform lighting.

Although free standing single and double lamps were produced, many were neatly incorporated into concrete panels bearing the station name and a pair of posters. Most stations received the hoop-and-globe type of lamp, as shown in the photo, right, outside Southgate. The globe was made from opal glass, and the concrete contained small stone chips to add interest to the colour and texture.

Uxbridge, Eastcote, East Finchley, Harrow-on-the-Hill, and some stations on the eastern extension of the Central line had their lamps suspended from curved concrete columns, Ruislip, Rayners Lane, Rickmansworth, Roding Valley, and Wembley Park all had bronze hemispheres containing the lamps, fixed into metal hoops, whilst Osterley and Oakwood were given unique designs. Boston and Ruislip Manor, although rebuilt by Holden, retained their wooden platform buildings and so no new lighting was provided.

Unfortunately, despite the attention to detail and the design integrating with the overall look of the stations, almost all of these lamps have been removed and replaced with modern high-pressure sodium lamps of bland design. Only Rayners Lane and Sudbury Town have kept their original 1930s-style lamps on the platforms. Roding Valley also retains a pair of its lights outside the station, as shown in the photograph. These have been fitted with modern compact fluorescent lamps in keeping with the Underground's energy reduction policy.

'Hoop-and-globe' lamp at Southgate, 1933

Roding Valley, 1949

The original lanterns on this 1948 structure were metal dishes. The modern replacements are less in keeping with the design.

Southgate has lighting integrated with the stepped ceiling at each entrance.

Turnpike Lane, 1932

Southgate, 1933

Arnos Grove, 1933

TRAIN SHEDS

In the early years of the twentieth century, many of the Metropolitan and District Railway stations had large roofs covering the platform areas. These were provided from the outset, and consisted of arched metal structures with glazing allowing light down to the platforms. Glazed screens at open ends of the roofs helped deflect some of the wind that would blow under them; typically only one end would be open, with the other being adjacent to the station building.

Much of the original Metropolitan Railway was located under streets, and it was only the stations at Edgware Road and King's Cross which were given these roofs. The extension east to the City had one at Barbican, and Farringdon had a pair of partially-glazed roofs over each pair of tracks.

Overall roofs were used at every station on the 1868 extension of the MR south and west from Edgware Road, to South Kensington. The MDR used very similar roofs in its stations east from the latter station to Charing Cross; only Westminster omitted the roof as it has buildings and gardens over much of the platform area.

The stations at King's Cross, Barbican, High Street Kensington, Gloucester Road, and South Kensington all had large roofs spanning four tracks and their platforms, but the roofs were removed from the latter three stations around 1907, when they were replaced by standard wooden canopies as part of station modernization schemes. King's Cross lost its roof in late 1911 when a road was constructed over the platforms, and wartime damage at Barbican led to its roof being removed in early 1955.

Of the arched roofs over two-track stations, those at Paddington and Notting Hill Gate remain in best condition. Bayswater has had most removed due to over-station development, and those at Edgware Road, Sloane Square, Victoria, St James's Park, and Charing Cross have all been removed. The supporting brackets for the roofs can still be seen at Barbican and Sloane Square; see p138.

Paddington retains three bays of its original 1868 train shed roof.

Earl's Court retains a different style of train shed, with an angled roof, which was constructed in 1878 when the station was moved to its current site. It extends most of the way along the platforms from the Earl's Court Road station building in the east, and is 340 ft (104 m) long. It was magnificently restored in 2009, giving the station a cleaner and brighter appearance. One station to the south, at West Brompton, there is a smaller roof covering the northern part of the District line platforms. This is unique, having a shallower arch than other stations and with a wooden screen at the southern end.

One final station retaining an original train shed is Aldgate, where the central part of the platforms is covered by an arched roof. This has similar glazing to the other MR stations, but different supporting ribs.

The largest train shed roof on the Underground is at Earl's Court, sheltering the District line platforms.

TUNNEL PORTALS

The point where the platform area meets the running tunnel is rarely considered by most passengers, but even here there are elements of design and difference between stations and lines.

It would appear from photographic evidence that the three earliest tube railways (the C&SLR, W&CR, and CLR) left the walls around their tunnel mouths unadorned, and it was the UERL which introduced the idea of decorating the end walls of their stations.

The first sign of decoration at the portals came with the opening of the Baker Street & Waterloo Railway in 1906. False stonework was placed around the portal with a radiating pattern between the 'blocks', forming a voussoir arch. This was used subsequently across the three tube lines owned by the UERL, although the central 'keystone' was made taller on Piccadilly and Hampstead line stations.

This style of portal continued with the extension of the Bakerloo line west from Baker Street, although the Piccadilly and Hampstead style was used.

A different, rather simpler style of tunnel portal decoration was used when the C&SLR was reconstructed with larger running tunnels in the early 1920s. A curved band around the top of the tunnel was created on the wall, with a 'keystone' projecting forward slightly. These can still be seen at some stations such as King's Cross. Similar 'keystones' were provided above the access passageways to the platforms. At some point since, the portals on the Northern line from Clapham North southwards have been altered, giving a double keystone with the centre stone rather more angled than the original. The curved band is also thinner.

An interesting feature at Arsenal, Holloway Road, and Caledonian Road stations, on the Piccadilly line, is the decorative painting of the tunnel portal surrounds, with alternate voussoirs in dark green and white.

Decoration of portals was mostly dropped after the 1920s extension southwards on the C&SLR. The 1930s Piccadilly line extension to Cockfosters featured just a thin band of coloured tiles over each portal.

Edgware Road (Bakerloo)

Clapham North

A rather more sinister style of portal was created from necessity at the start of the Second World War. Fear that a German bomb could breach one of the tunnels passing beneath the Thames led to the installation of floodgates at several stations, allowing the tunnels to be sealed off. The decorative stonework from 1906 has been removed, and a metal frame installed which seals tightly against a sliding metal door.

Just before the war a programme of platform lengthening had commenced on the Bakerloo line, so that longer trains could be operated. This meant opening out sections of running tunnel adjacent to one end of each platform and extending the platform and decoration into the new, larger tunnel. Decorative finishes were not applied to the new portals. Likewise, the portals on the new platforms at Swiss Cottage and St John's Wood were left plain, and slightly recessed behind a squared-off opening.

Subsequent tunnel portals have been left plain, generally appearing as just dark holes with straight edges along the top and platform side with the curved tunnel section recessed further making it hard to see.

Refurbishment of older stations has seen some of the original decorative portals removed. In their place a variety of décor has been used, ranging from plain walls, small plastered 'lips', narrow painted bands, and rings of tiles. Where the UERL voussoir surrounds have remained is inconsistent, many platforms just retaining them at one end. On the Bakerloo line this is because of the extension of the platforms in the 1930s, with the voussoirs not usually replaced on the portals at the extended ends. They have been painted in various colours, white tending to hide them at refurbished stations, green highlighting them, and at the three Piccadilly line stations east of King's Cross, green and white for alternate voussoirs.

King's Cross St Pancras (Northern)

Wood Green

MISCELLANY

There are many heritage features around the Underground which do not fit into neat categories. These pages show a selection that can still be found by the observant passenger.

The 'Archer' at East Finchley aims his imaginary arrow at the heart of London, representing the rapid travel brought to the station in 1939 with the coming of the Underground. It is made of a wooden frame covered in sheet lead, and was created by Eric Aumonier.

The centre tracks at East Finchley were served by steam trains until 1964, when the goods yard at Mill Hill East closed. Smoke deflectors were cast into the concrete lintel of the building to reduce the effects of the smoke entering the windows.

This wooden milepost, dating back to the Metropolitan Railway, marks the spot four miles from Baker Street, on the disused northbound platform at Willesden Green.

The gutter header boxes along the platforms at Becontree are embossed with the year of manufacture. These are also at Upminster, Hornchurch, and other stations on the eastern branch of the District line, but only those at Becontree are painted this way. Becontree was rebuilt in 1931/2 from a small halt.

The spiral stair shaft at Tufnell Park is unlined, allowing the manufacturer's mark to be seen. HW & Co Ltd were Head Wrightson of Teesside, 18-0 is the diameter (18 ft 0 ins), and UERCL is the Underground Electric Railway Company of London.

The Metropolitan Railway monogram can be seen in these grilles along the passageway leading to the footbridge over the Circle line platforms at Baker Street.

The offices above Edgware Road station are reached by a side door, above which is an attractive porthole window. The offices are called Edgware House. These form part of the 1926 station designed by C. W. Clark.

Many of the bronze staircase handrails around the Underground have still been retained. This is at Acton Town.

This tiled pillar, incorporating poster frames and lighting is at Turnpike Lane station, and is in keeping with the Art Deco design of the 1930s.

Southgate was built with a unique 'pylon' above the station roof, resembling an electrical insulator. It forms a distinctive local landmark.

South Woodford retains an etched glass window from its days as a Great Eastern Railway station. The window is a carefully made replica, with the original in store for the London Transport Museum, following concerns about possible damage. Similar windows at Buckhurst Hill were broken by vandals in 1995, and replicas were provided.

Sloane Square used to have a glazed, arched roof over the platforms. It was destroyed by a bomb in 1940, and the only traces remaining today are the metal brackets that can be seen set into the brick retaining wall above the modern platform canopy. Similar brackets remain at Barbican, where the roof was also removed following wartime damage.

Far left: The westbound platform at East Ham still has a pair of painted advertisements for, presumably, a refreshment room. They are just beneath the girders supporting the canopy either side of where a doorway has been bricked up.

Left: Many of the stations designed by Charles Holden incorporated matching concrete fencing along their platforms. In many cases this has become broken, or the concrete has spalled from the interal reinforcement bars, but at Rayners Lane it remains substantially intact along both platforms.

Wooden escalators, once standard on the Underground, can now be found only at the open air station Greenford, where they connect the street level booking area with the elevated platforms.

White City retains a roundel sign incorporating a fluorescent lamp at each end of each of its platforms. These lights date back to the station opening in 1947, and are some of the oldest original lamps on the Underground.

Rickmansworth retains one of the few water towers remaining on the Underground. From 1925 until 1960 this was used by the steam locomotives hauling trains north-west to Aylesbury and beyond.

A surprisingly large number of stations retain this early design of signal as their platform repeater (i.e., repeating the signal that the driver sees). The design is unchanged since its introduction on the UERL tubes around 1910, and because of the shape they are known to staff as 'coffee pots'. This example is at Balham.

Leicester Square station carries evidence of offices above it once being occupied by publishers of the famous cricketing annual.

Temple station has this map dating from 1932 just outside the entrance. It has been preserved as an item of historical interest.

Uxbridge was opened in 1938 with this attractive stained glass window, which was designed by Ervin Bossányi. It features the coat of arms of Uxbridge Urban District Council flanked by those of the counties of Buckinghamshire and Middlesex.

Barons Court, 1905

Farringdon, 1923

One of the most unusual items of Underground architecture is actually a work of art by Eduardo Paolozzi (see also the Tottenham Court Road mosaics, p37–8). In 1982 he completed a commission to decorate a new shaft providing ventilation from the Victoria line station. The shaft is clad on all four sides with cast iron panels decorated with raised pictures of... well, all sorts of things. Butterflies, girders, fish, gauges, polygons... the list goes on, although careful inspection reveals that there is a repeated set of items, but in different arrangements on each side. Three of the sides are each composed of six panels; the other has a pair of full-height doors, but these do not cut across any of the décor. The side facing Bessborough Street includes two small panels featuring the names of Paolozzi and the manufacturer, R. Watson.

INDEX

Note: There may be more than one reference on the page indicated. Photographs have references in *italics*. Stations with listed status have this noted in square brackets after their name. The following grades of listing are shown, the first three being awarded by English Heritage for buildings of national interest:

Grade 1, the highest level of protection
Grade 2★, for particularly important buildings
Grade 2, for buildings of special interest
L: Buildings listed by the relevant Local Authority
a4: Protected under Article 4(1) of the Town and Country Planning (General Permitted Development) Order 1995

† is used to indicate where only part of a station is covered by the listing.
Barkingside, Loughton, Moorgate†, and Park Royal stations are also Grade 2 listed, but do not feature in this book.
For further information about Underground heritage, please visit http://undergroundheritage.wordpress.com.